To be
the Church

Konrad Raiser

To be the Church

Challenges and Hopes for a New Millennium

WCC Publications, Geneva

Cover design: Edwin Hassink
Cover illustration: Johan van der Noort

ISBN 2-8254-1211-2

© 1997 WCC Publications, World Council of Churches,
150 route de Ferney, 1211 Geneva 2, Switzerland

No. 78 in the Risk Book Series

Printed in Switzerland

TO ELISABETH,
COMPANION AND CO-WORKER

Table of Contents

Introduction

Only a few years separate us from the beginning of the 21st century. But this "turn of the century" is a special one, for we are also on the eve of a new millennium. Its arrival is being anticipated with a variety of expectations, hopes and fears by religious leaders and ordinary people, enthusiastic futurists and prophets of doom, academics and journalists, cultural figures and government officials. Most keenly, perhaps, the coming change of the calendar has been noted in the business world, where it has been recognized for some time already that attaching the figure "2000" to the name of a product can give it the irresistible allure of being ahead of its time.

Experts warn that financial chaos looms if computer programmes now operating are not altered to enable the large mainframes that regulate payments, pensions and taxes to distinguish the year 2000 from the year 1900. Travel agents have done a lively business in selling package tours for New Year's Eve 1999 on islands in the South Pacific where, according to our way of reckoning time, the year 2000 will first dawn on planet earth.

Within the Christian community, many evangelistic organizations have taken the year 2000 as the focal point of energetic new campaigns to proclaim the gospel in every part of the world. Other Christians, clearly influenced by the imagery of the "thousand years" in Revelation 20, entertain dramatic, even apocalyptic expectations and anxieties about the beginning of a new millennium. Meanwhile, the argument remains unresolved as to whether the beginning of that new millennium and the new century ought to be marked on 1 January 2000 or 1 January 2001.

In the face of all this, some would speak a note of caution, a reminder that our means of specifying dates and times are a matter of convention, not something built into the fabric of reality. In particular, the designation of the year 2000 on the calendar that is used almost universally today depends on a calculation — now widely considered to have been erroneous — of the date of the birth of Jesus. If the year indicated by a round number like 2000 is judged significant around the world (and 2000 is of course a "round number" only because of the conventional use of the decimal system in counting), it is because of the global dominance in recent centuries of a civilization whose religious identity was shaped by faith in Jesus Christ. This is tacitly acknowledged in the increasing use of the abbreviations "B.C.E." and "C.E." — "Before the Common Era" and "Common Era" — in place of "B.C.", "before Christ", and "A.D.", *Anno Domino*, "in the year of our Lord".

This counsel of caution about attaching mystical significance to dates, however, does not detract from the importance most religious traditions give to setting aside specific dates and times to reflect in community about the past, the present and the future. In many Christian traditions, the liturgical year provides a cycle of opportunities for such commemoration and reflection. So, too, the approach of the year 2000 may serve as an opportunity for common reflection.

From the point of view of the church as a whole, the thousand-year period now coming to an end could be described as the millennium of Christian division. Two dates especially symbolize this: the year 1054, when the mutual excommunications between Rome and Constantinople sealed a split between Western and Eastern Christianity whose consequences have endured to this day; and 1517, when the best-known of the reform movements which touched off centuries of fragmentation within the Western church began with Martin Luther's posting of his 95 theses.

Both of these symbolic moments of division happened in Europe. Their consequences, however, did not remain in Europe. The missionary movement exported divisions within Christianity to every part of the world, usually in complete disregard of the specifically European historical and contextual factors that had created or aggravated them. The continuing effects which this had on Christian mission and on the Christian church and Christian community in every part of the world are well-known. We need not dwell on them here, except as a reminder that it is important, in looking back at history, to be aware of the standpoint from which one is looking — as the commemorations in 1992 of the 500th anniversary of the voyage of Christopher Columbus illustrated.

The year 2000, however, marks the end not only of a millennium, but also of a century. And if one can in broad strokes sketch the second millennium as the millennium of Christian division, one might equally describe the 20th century in terms of the quest for Christian unity. Indeed, the term given to this phenomenon, the "ecumenical movement", is often used with the adjective "20th-century". Again, a few representative dates stand out: 1910, the year of the great world missionary conference in Edinburgh, which many historians have described as the birthplace of the ecumenical movement; 1948, the year of the founding assembly of the World Council of Churches in Amsterdam; and 1962, the year of the beginning of the Second Vatican Council, whose decisions over the course of the next three years brought the Roman Catholic Church fully into the ecumenical movement, from which it had previously maintained a critical distance. Again, important nuances must be noted to this sweeping portrait of our century: the fact that there were significant efforts to restore the visible unity of the church before the 20th century; and the acknowledgment that, influential though it has been, the ecumenical vision has been kept alive by a minority within the churches.

Founded in 1948, the World Council of Churches, which has been the most prominent international expression of the ecumenical movement, will thus mark its own 50th anniversary shortly before the end of this "ecumenical century". The culmination of this commemoration will take place at the Council's eighth assembly in Harare, Zimbabwe, in December 1998. As we shall discuss in more detail later, the planning for this assembly has sought on the one hand to reclaim the biblical idea of jubilee (Leviticus 25) — the source of the ordinary use of this word to describe any significant anniversary, but especially a fiftieth anniversary — and on the other hand to provide the churches an opportunity, on the eve of a new millennium, a new century and a new period in the life of the WCC, to recommit themselves to the ecumenical vision.

Of all that has been written and said about the 20th-century ecumenical movement, one of the most often quoted remarks is that made by William Temple in 1942 at his enthronement as Archbishop of Canterbury and primate of the Church of England. The great ecumenical pioneer, whose untimely death in 1944 prevented him from seeing the completion of the process of formation of the World Council, whose provisional committee he had chaired from its start in 1938, described the "worldwide fellowship of Christians" as the "great new fact of our era".

Half a century later, there are probably few even among the most committed church members who would characterize the ecumenical movement in such terms. Most Christians in the 1990s, asked to identify the "great new facts" of our time, would likely mention the technological progress symbolized by computers and the mass media of communication; or perhaps such political and economic developments as the end of the cold war and the "globalization" of the market economy. Others of a more philosophical bent might speak of "post-modernism" or the "end of ideology" or, looking ahead, the "coming clash of civilizations".

For the great majority of church members, it is safe to say, the eclipse of the idea of the ecumenical movement as a decisive and significant reality of our time is not a matter of hostility to its aims or even to the activities undertaken by its institutional expressions during the 20th century. Rather, most are probably unaware of the work of the ecumenical movement and take its achievements for granted and its reverses as unimportant.

The churches that were most active in the movement which led to the founding of the World Council of Churches in 1948 have often been characterized as the "historic churches". In certain countries, this status took the shape of some kind of "establishment", an official identification of the church with the state. Elsewhere, they were "folk churches", understood to be the virtual monopoly form of the Christian faith in their country. These were churches with a long history and a conscious awareness of their tradition. Even in the United States of America, where the separation of church and state was a principle explicitly enshrined in the nation's constitution from the beginning, these churches, predominantly Protestant, were thought of as the "mainline churches".

Today, the reality is quite different. While church membership statistics are usually imprecise and always difficult to compare and to interpret, it is generally agreed that the total membership of the member churches of the World Council of Churches is less than half of the total membership of the Roman Catholic Church, which is not a member of the WCC. More pertinently, statistics suggest that within a very short time, if not already, the membership of WCC member churches will include fewer than half of *the non-Roman Catholic Christians* in the world. The astonishing numerical growth of many churches which have not been part of the 20th-century movement for the visible unity of the church — Pentecostal groups in Latin America, indigenous churches not linked with any of the historic European Christian traditions, especially in Africa, independent and largely congregation-based evangelical churches in North America — suggests that this minority status of the churches which provided the central impetus for the ecumenical movement will continue.

To be sure, the strength and vitality of the church, and thus of the ecumenical movement as a fellowship of churches, is not to be measured solely or even primarily in numerical terms. Nor should participation in the ecumenical movement be equated with membership of the traditional organizational forms which the quest for the unity of the church has taken in the latter half of the 20th century. Around the world a lively variety of ecumenical activity is taking place, especially at the local level, animated by individuals and groups and congregations who may never use the word "ecumenical".

Nevertheless, it is clear that, as the "ecumenical century" recedes into history and as the most visible global manifestation of that movement — the World Council of Churches — celebrates its 50th anniversary, a rekindling of the vision is needed. It is this need which has given rise during the 1990s to a process of study and consultation "Towards a Common Understanding and Vision of the World Council of Churches". It is hoped that this study will culminate in a kind of new ecumenical charter which the churches can affirm as the new millennium approaches.

Such a charter must seek to do justice to the convictions and needs of churches from a wide variety of cultures and traditions and from every part of the world. It must respond to their perceptions of the challenges confronting humanity at this point in history. It must continue and revitalize the heritage of the several streams of ecumenical engagement that flowed together into the WCC in 1948 and thereafter — to overcome differences of theology and church order, to offer a common witness in a divided world, to address human needs in a world of injustice, violence and environmental destruction, to foster the growth of an ecumenical consciousness and a vision of life in community rooted in each particular context. It must draw on the lessons of fifty years of life together within the WCC to discern the challenges we face, the resources we have and the convictions we share.

The need to rekindle the ecumenical vision is the concern behind this short book. The life of the World Council of Churches itself forms the immediate context out of which it is written. This is not to suggest that the World Council of Churches is the supreme expression or even the most important instrument of the ecumenical movement; to make such a claim would be to go against the very identity of the WCC as a *fellowship of churches*. But the WCC is and is likely to remain the broadest and most inclusive — both in terms of its global scope and its openness to churches from all Christian traditions — among the many bodies which together form one ecumenical movement. And it is the organization with which I am most familiar, having been privileged to serve on its staff for nearly 20 years, between 1969 and 1983 and again since 1993.

Because the ecumenical movement has been a movement of churches, this book begins its reflections on the search for a renewed ecumenical vision by listening to some of the voices that are coming from the churches in the WCC at this point in history. Chapter 1 draws largely on the visits I have made to WCC member churches since I began my service as general secretary of the WCC in 1993. It is thus not a scientific survey, but an attempt to hear and reflect what the churches now involved in the ecumenical movement are saying — and not saying — about that commitment.

The churches in the ecumenical movement are churches that live in the world. Chapter 2 therefore attempts to distill some of the challenges to the churches emerging from the vast and rapid changes that have become evident in our world in the years since the WCC was founded. In the face of the contemporary form of universal unity that goes under the name "globalization", it explores the Christian visions of catholicity and conciliarity. Reflecting in particular on the experience of the WCC's "conciliar process for justice, peace and the integrity of creation" in the 1980s, I attempt to identify the implications of this in the new global context at the dawn of the new millennium, linking the idea of conciliarity with recent discussions of "civil society".

A common source and resource of the ecumenical movement has been the Bible. Studying the Bible together across the traditional lines of division among the churches was the dynamic of those mission-oriented student movements of the late 19th and early 20th centuries which proved to be the crucible of the ecumenical movement. In many countries, the work of the Bible societies in translating and distributing Scripture has been one of the most successful manifestations of ecumenical commitment. The role of the Bible as a common source and resource for the divided churches was recognized in the addition of the words "according to the Scriptures" in the Basis of the WCC by the New Delhi assembly in 1961; and regular daily Bible study is a central facet of all World Council meetings from small consultations to assemblies. Chapters 3-5 thus look at a renewed ecumenical vision in terms of biblical images. Chapter 3 suggests several biblical orientations to the future which have animated ecumenical commitment in recent years. Chapters 4 and 5 elaborate one biblical vision, the vision of jubilee, in terms of the theme of the WCC's eighth assembly: "Turn to God — Rejoice in Hope".

Finally, chapter 6 suggests some of the practical implications of this vision in terms of creating an ecumenical movement that is equipped to respond to the challenges of a new millennium.

The title of this book draws on some memorable and challenging words from the German ecumenist Ernst Lange (1927-74), in his book *And Yet It Moves*.... Describing ecumenism as "the test case of faith", Lange wrote that "today, there is... only one way for the church to be the one, holy, catholic and apostolic church, and that is the ecumenical way". This insight seems to me to be even more pertinent now than when Lange wrote these words 25 years ago.

The pages that follow explore some of the facets of what "the ecumenical way" might mean in the 21st century. This book is not, therefore, intended as a full theological treatment of the church and its nature; indeed, it is written out of the recognition that our differences on this point are never too far below the surface of our ecumenical encounter and that they pose one of the major obstacles to our discerning together "the ecumenical way". It is also written against the background of an intensified discussion of the meaning of ecumenism in the context of the process "Towards a Common Understanding and Vision of the World Council of Churches"; and many of the issues being raised by the WCC's member churches and ecumenical partners in the course of that discussion find an echo in these pages, including (especially in chapter 6) questions about the institutional form of the WCC. But my purpose here is not to make definite proposals in these areas, nor to deal in depth with the specific activities which a freshly re-visioned Council might undertake. Instead, this book seeks to point to important questions, stimulate a readiness to push beyond where we have come, imagine a different future and hint at some of the ways in which the ecumenical movement and the bodies that serve it might recapture the élan and relevance which warranted Archbishop Temple's enthusiastic commendation of it as "the great new fact of our time".

1. Voices from the Churches

All local pastors are aware of the expectations of their parishioners to be visited personally. Since time constraints usually oblige pastors with large congregations to limit such calls to moments of crisis in the life of individual members or families, they often enlist the volunteer services of lay members of the congregation to share in this responsibility through regular visits to those who are old, lonely or in some other need. But such visits are generally considered less significant than a personal call by the pastor.

Beyond the level of the local worshipping community, all churches regard visitation as one of the essential responsibilities of bishops or others entrusted with the ministry of oversight. Not only does this include periodic formal visits to congregations or church districts, but it also involves regular pastoral care for those who are themselves leaders of local communities. This *mutuum colloquium fratrum* — speaking together as brothers and sisters to share concerns and problems, joys and anxieties, convictions and doubts — does not follow the bureaucratic logic of "performance appraisals"; rather, it is the elemental form of conciliar life in the church. It takes time to build such relationships to the point that a real process of entering into spiritual communion with one another can occur.

Living letters

What is true of the local parish and of a given church in its national or denominational form also applies ecumenically to the broader relations of the churches. Visiting each other has been, since the time of St Paul, an important means of strengthening mutual relationships and thus maintaining the sense of the catholicity of the church. When travel over long distances was time-consuming and difficult, such mutual visits were exceptional moments of great importance. This was still the case in the early days of the ecumenical movement. To a great extent, the worldwide networks of the Student Christian Movement and later of the International Missionary Council were built through the extensive journeys undertaken by John R. Mott to visit Christian communities in what were for him the remotest parts of the world. These occasions remained in the memory of the visitors and the visited for a long time.

Air travel and ever more rapid means of communication have radically intensified the quantity of interchurch encounters. Letters are routinely exchanged, increasingly by electronic means. International meetings and consultations have become an ordinary instrument of ecumenical work. Many ecumenical staff persons spend considerable time travelling to visit partners in churches and church agencies. But as this network of relationships has become wider and the contacts more regular, much of the special quality of the earlier visits has been lost. Visits have become functional, leaving little room for a genuine meeting of minds and sharing of experiences.

After the WCC's fifth assembly (Nairobi 1975), its office on Renewal and Congregational Life worked out a strategy of sending ecumenical teams to member churches and their congregations to stimulate ecumenical learning and strengthen relationships among churches. In 1979, one such team made an extensive visit to the churches in what was then the German Democratic Republic. The experience left a lasting mark both on those visited and on the ten members of the team. The team sent an "open letter" to the East German churches after the visit, giving an account of what they had seen and heard. It was widely discussed; and this influenced ecumenical developments in the GDR over the next decade, up to the large assemblies on Justice, Peace and Integrity of Creation organized by the churches there in 1988 and 1989. But even more important than this open letter were the many profound and moving encounters during the visit itself. These came to be seen as a contemporary example of the sending of "living letters" — "written not with ink but with the Spirit of the living God, not on tablets of stone but on tables of human hearts" (2 Cor. 3:3).

Inspired by the experience of this visit, the WCC in 1981 undertook a comprehensive effort to send ecumenical teams to as many of its churches as possible during the two years before its next assembly in Vancouver in 1983. Most of the teams included persons who would be delegates to the assembly from churches elsewhere as well as members of WCC governing and advisory bodies and staff. They met with church leaders and members of local congregations, seminary students and faculty, staff of church institutions, civil authorities and others. Hospitality in private homes offered many of the ecumenical visitors an occasion for personal encounter and sharing in the everyday life of a Christian family in a country distant and different from their own. Most of these visits created unique and moving experiences of communion in the same faith across boundaries of race, class, culture and language.

Long after the Vancouver assembly, these visits were cited as the WCC's most significant initiative to deepen relationships with and among its member churches; and team visits to express pastoral concern for and Christian solidarity with churches facing challenges of many different types have become a regular element of the WCC's life and work. In 1994 another comprehensive effort to visit all WCC member churches began, this time around the specific issues raised by the WCC's Ecumenical Decade — Churches in Solidarity with Women, again using the theme of "living letters".

Impressions from the churches

Since the general secretary of the WCC is responsible not only for the work of the staff in the central office in Geneva but also to represent the Council as a fellowship of churches, maintaining and developing relationships with member churches and other ecumenical partners is an essential part of the task. Thus when I assumed this position in January 1993, I committed myself to visiting as many member churches as possible during my first years in office. Over the past four years, I have been able to visit nearly half of the WCC's 330 member churches in all regions of the world. In a number of cases this was the first official visit to a church by a general secretary of the WCC and was gratefully acknowledged as a symbol of belonging to a wider community, of not being disregarded or forgotten. This was particularly true among small member churches with limited means for maintaining international contacts and often living in a minority situation.

Following the model of ecumenical team visits, I was accompanied by two or three staff colleagues and sometimes a WCC central committee member from the region visited. We took part in worship, preached or brought greetings in Pentecostal communities in Zimbabwe, Chile and Korea, in Orthodox churches in Syria, Constantinople and Armenia, in Moravian congregations in Nicaragua and the USA, among Dalit Christians in India and indigenous Christians in Bolivia, in ecumenical services in China, Papua New Guinea, Vanuatu and Denmark, and in numerous Lutheran, Methodist, Anglican, Baptist and Presbyterian congregations all over the world. There have been intensive moments of sharing with heads of churches, church councils and parish groups, including groups of women and young people. I have lectured in theological faculties and seminaries, visited monasteries, hospitals, schools, media centres, agricultural projects and centres for adult education, and met with ecumenical organizations and councils of churches. Most visits have included contacts with civic groups working on human rights, refugee problems, environmental issues or popular education, as well as heads of state or government leaders.

It has been a unique privilege to experience in this way the richness and diversity of the life of the churches in all parts of the world, to sense first hand the real communion which exists between Christians of different cultures and traditions as ecumenical visitors are received as brothers and sisters belonging to the same extended family.

As manifestations of the fellowship within the community of the WCC, such visits are essentially pastoral in character, not in the sense of exercising oversight — for the WCC has no authority over its member churches — but as an expression of caring concern for the life and witness of the member churches and of a readiness to reflect with those in positions of leadership about the meaning and implications of their church's membership in the World Council.

What do church leaders and those responsible for particular areas of work in a given church share with the general secretary of the WCC during a visit? While generalizations are hardly possible, since the churches live and work and witness under such very different circumstances, some impressions do stand out.

An initial general — and sobering — observation is that for many member churches, particularly in the southern hemisphere, the World Council of Churches is a distant organization about which they know very little. Despite regular letters to all member churches and other efforts to convey information about the Council's work, churches appear to have difficulty developing a sense of belonging to a community of churches through the WCC. In many traditional cultures, only oral communication in a face-to-face meeting can establish a relationship. Information provided in written or printed form, especially if it does not relate to the immediate concerns of the churches, has little effect. In churches whose central offices have a very small staff, official correspondence and other materials sent from Geneva seldom reach beyond the desk of the first person to receive them. Thus during visits to many churches I discovered that the staff persons responsible for theological education or women's work or lay training knew little or nothing about the activities of the WCC in their respective areas, even though a great deal of information had been sent to their church. Sometimes one of the barriers seems to be a traditional hierarchical understanding of leadership, which does not include the practice of regularly sharing or passing on information. But even when information is shared, those receiving it often do not know what to do with it. All of these difficulties are magnified if the church does not have staff who can communicate comfortably in one of the four languages in which the WCC regularly works — English, French, German and Spanish.

Even members of the WCC central committee, who are directly involved in the Council's work and receive regular and ample information about it, often seem able to do little by way of sharing this knowledge and experience with responsible leaders in their church and the other churches of their country. Belonging to a governing body of the WCC seems almost unrelated to their work at home. The WCC's commitment to ensure the presence of women, young people and lay persons on its central committee only adds to this difficulty, for unless these people have a recognized place in the structures of their church, their ability to serve as channels of communication in both directions is severely limited.

Given this communication gap built into the very structure of the WCC, it is little wonder that many churches look on it as one of those "service agencies" in the rich West from which assistance and support are available. Many churches assess the importance of their relationships with the WCC on the basis of the services the Council can offer in response to their immediate needs; and, since the WCC is not the only agency available, it must sometimes prove its relevance in competition with others. Even churches which have highly valued the ecumenical solidarity and support coming through the WCC during times of oppression may turn indifferent once the oppressive situation has changed. Sometimes churches complain that they are not receiving what they consider their "fair share" of outside support in comparison with those who have privileged contacts with ecumenical partners.

This almost utilitarian way of looking at the WCC relates not only to its involvement in resource-sharing. It is also reflected in the way many member churches perceive the programmatic work of the Council — as activities undertaken by an organization which sets and follows its own policies. Where these activities respond to concerns which are high on its own agenda, a church may show interest, active support or critical concern about them. But since the WCC develops and carries out many of its activities in cooperation with particular groups or individuals in the constituency, the churches as such — which are the member bodies of the WCC — may feel only slight involvement. With some notable exceptions, WCC activities appear to contribute little to the deepening of ecumenical awareness among the churches, their leaders and the people in the congregations. As a result, there is often little or no response to recommendations to the churches arising out of the work of the WCC or requests to them for implementation or follow-up or even information about what they are doing.

The situation is somewhat different in the case of churches, chiefly the Council's large member churches, which structure their own programmatic activities in a way that more or less parallels the WCC's various areas of work. Throughout its nearly fifty years of existence, the WCC has received its main financial support from this group of "historic Protestant" churches. But most of these churches have recently faced severe internal crises manifested in an erosion of membership and a decline of financial resources. With the majority of their energies devoted to maintaining their own institutional integrity, they are finding less and less space for ecumenical involvement.

In reflecting, as they must, on what it means to be the church today, all these churches realize that painful processes of de-institutionalization may lie ahead of them. But while it would seem obvious that they should be seeking the response to this question together and not separately, the ecumenical dimension of this challenge has not yet been addressed adequately. At the same time, many of these churches have built up an intensive network of interchurch relationships, sometimes leading to the establishment of full communion among them through such instruments as the Leuenberg and Porvoo Agreements in Europe, or various schemes now before the churches in the United States. This new level of ecumenical relationships has a profound significance at least for the place of Protestant churches in the ecumenical movement. So far, however, it has not been reflected in the self-understanding of the World Council of Churches as a fellowship of churches, for all these churches continue to be represented there as individual, "sovereign" bodies, as though their ecumenical relations outside the WCC had no implications for their membership of the Council.

Dominant concerns

As I meet with persons in leadership positions in the churches, particularly in the South, a few needs and concerns are mentioned again and again. These priorities naturally shape their expectations regarding the agenda of the WCC. At the top of the list in many of these meetings are the concerns for evangelism and education. The two are closely related. Most churches have a shortage of people qualified to carry on the work of evangelism: spreading the gospel, nurturing the faith of the newly converted through Christian education, reaching out both to those who are seekers of the faith and to those who have moved away from the church and have become indifferent. Linked with these priority areas is a growing interest among the churches in using modern media of mass communication for the purposes of evangelism and Christian nurture. To be present in the media, especially radio and television, which reach into nearly every home, has become an urgent concern of the churches today; and many look to the World Council of Churches as a source of advice and training, a place to exchange experiences with other churches and a source of material support.

In many of the places I have visited, the churches' concern about evangelism is related to the growing influence in their context of "sects" and new religious movements. The stories told are very similar from Russia to the Pacific, from Egypt to South Africa: the churches are disturbed by a massive influx of either Christian charismatic and fundamentalist groups or movements of a syncretistic religious character, and by the aggressive methods of recruitment they use. Appealing to the principles of religious liberty, these groups engage in what the local churches consider to be proselytism, especially among young people still in the formative stage of their identity. Some of the Christian groups coming in are virulently anti-ecumenical. This creates embarrassment and confusion among WCC member churches and their leaders, who feel at a loss to correct the distorted image of ecumenism. Lacking information, experience, qualified people or resources, they are unable to confront and engage these groups by presenting a strong gospel message. Some have become defensive and turn to the government for protection.

This raises the further issue of church-state relationships, a key concern in my visits to churches in formerly socialist countries in Europe (Russia, Poland), Latin America (Argentina, Bolivia, Chile) and China. Often this concern crystallizes around the discussion of constitutional amendments or the drafting of new constitutions, particularly the question of how to ensure equality of legal status for majority and minority churches. But the issue of the public recognition and role of churches and religious communities is being debated in many countries. Does the demand by governments for registration of religious communities infringe upon religious liberty? What kind of access should churches and other religious communities have to public educational institutions and the media? Should a particular interpretation of Christian moral values be incorporated in the constitution? More and more churches are looking to ecumenical bodies and other churches in the ecumenical community for advice on such issues, since they feel unable by themselves to address the questions involved and to defend their interests.

A dominant issue in many of my conversations with leaders of WCC member churches is the relationship of their church to other churches on the national level, especially with the Roman Catholic Church or with Pentecostal churches. This is a particular concern for small churches belonging to one of the historic Protestant denominations, but it raises more general questions about ecumenical relations between the churches in the same country.

The rules of the World Council express the expectation that its member churches will "recognize the essential interdependence of the churches" and "practise constructive ecumenical relations with other churches within [their] country or region. This will normally mean that the church is a member of the national council of churches or similar body and of the regional ecumenical organization." Behind this rule lies the conviction that membership of the WCC which is not matched by "constructive ecumenical relations" at home loses its base. It is in the local and national context that the ecumenical commitment of the churches is put to the test.

Few WCC member churches would disagree with this principle. But the reality of relationships between churches in the same country often speaks a different language. Leaders of many councils of churches have in their turn expressed concern about what they perceive as a renewed affirmation of denominational identity among the churches of their country or region. This encourages competitiveness among the churches and the cultivation of bilateral links with partners outside the country or region rather than cooperation among the churches. As a result, the national ecumenical body is weak. Its structures are minimal and its activities limited. Often it may serve as nothing more than a forum for meetings of leaders of the different churches and for the representation of common interests over against the government.

Among national and regional ecumenical bodies which are modelled on the WCC and thus have a larger institutional structure, many also find themselves in difficulties. Outside funding has declined or has been redirected to other agencies, obliging them to cut back their activities and to mobilize a renewed commitment among their member churches, including financial support.

Some have concluded that their existing base of support among the churches in their country or region is too limited to allow them to serve as a genuine catalyst for ecumenical relations. In response to this, two tendencies have become visible: (1) an effort to integrate the Roman Catholic Church, as in the United Kingdom, Australia, Aotearoa New Zealand, South Africa and more than forty other national ecumenical bodies, as well as the regional organizations in the Pacific, the Middle East and the Caribbean; (2) an effort to win the support of the large evangelical and Pentecostal churches, as in Korea and Latin America. In some countries — France and Argentina, for example — a Protestant or Evangelical body and an ecumenical structure which includes the Roman Catholic and Orthodox churches exist alongside each other.

By itself, creating a broader base for the national or regional ecumenical body does not necessarily strengthen the churches' willingness to cooperate with each other and to deepen their fellowship. Many church leaders do clearly recognize that the challenges lying ahead can be faced only by the churches together, that denominational defensiveness is not a viable option in a situation of increasing plurality. But as with all institutions, many churches and church bodies find themselves locked into structures which resist change, even if it is called for by basic theological agreement.

The strengthening of ecumenical relations on the local, national and regional levels is decisive for the future of the WCC. Most national ecumenical bodies and the seven regional ecumenical organizations are associated with the WCC, although their membership is generally wider, with a growing number including the Roman Catholic, Evangelical and Pentecostal churches. Training capable ecumenical leadership and building capacity on the national level must become a priority. An encouraging step in this direction is the initiative approved by the 1995 assembly of the Latin American Council of Churches to launch a comprehensive ecumenical youth leadership training programme.

The importance of this is underscored by the situation created in many countries by the new geopolitical constellation after the end of the cold war, the resolution of protracted armed conflicts in countries of Central America, Namibia and Mozambique, the abolition of repressive non-democratic regimes in South Africa, Chile, Korea and Taiwan, and the imposition of neo-liberal economic policies by the international financial institutions (as in the Caribbean, Ghana and Argentina). The new generation — and in many countries people under 25 are now the majority of the population — has new issues and new expectations. Their problems focus on unemployment, drugs, HIV-AIDS, gang violence and the situation of street children. Disillusioned by unfulfilled promises of easy material success, some are tempted to use violent means to obtain what society seems to be withholding from them.

At the same time, there is among this young generation a renewed interest in religious experience. In Latin America young people are reported to be returning to the church, having lost interest in old political confrontations and confidence in the formal political process. Their claim to space in the church is rooted in an understanding of life which is shaped less by social and political interests than by the dimensions of ecology, spirituality and faith. Similar observations were shared with me in Korea.

None of the churches can face these challenges alone. The familiar lines of confrontation and conflict which marked past decades are fast disappearing. Efforts in any country to establish a new democratic culture change the role of both the churches and the ecumenical movements at the grassroots. They must now find their place and redefine their identity in the context of an emerging civil society and in competition with newly established non-governmental organizations.

Heads of state and government leaders with whom I have spoken have expressed an urgent expectation for the churches to engage themselves in rebuilding the moral fabric of society. A critical dimension of this is educating people for citizenship — of which the initiative in the area of education for democracy taken by the churches in South Africa before the post-apartheid free elections in 1994 is a model. In many countries such education would have to include the reintegration into society of demobilized soldiers and resistance fighters.

Not surprisingly, churches are finding it difficult to respond to these and other new challenges posed by the new situation. In the past, many discovered the strength and value of ecumenical commitment and solidarity when they were resisting oppressive regimes. Today, when the challenge is to participate in the reconstruction of their societies, churches are often tempted instead to withdraw into themselves, reassert their traditional identity and fall back on the imagined security of "the way we have always done it". To be sure, this reluctance to change may reflect a sturdy commitment to the values and insights forged over centuries of Christian life and witness — a genuine desire to maintain the apostolic tradition. But too often it seems instead to be a concession to the pervasive consumer mentality of our time, in which a church sees its own beliefs and practices, forms of work and style of community as just one more product to be marketed successfully. Other churches are then viewed not as partners in the one ecumenical movement but as competitors for the same customers.

What does ecumenism mean?

But if it is true that being the church amidst the new challenges of our time can only mean being the church ecumenically, it is important to acknowledge that there is widespread uncertainty about — and even conflict over — the understanding of ecumenism today. This reality has been evident to me on my visits to the Pacific and South Africa, to Poland and England, to Aotearoa New Zealand and Latin America, to India and the Caribbean. And even though specific local factors and histories give this conflict about ecumenism different shapes and different accents in different places, the questions being raised are central ones for the future of the World Council of Churches and the ecumenical movement as a whole.

One example is the three different perspectives I heard emerging from an intensive debate on the future of ecumenism at the third assembly of the Latin American Council of Churches in 1995. There is, first, the question of the future of classical ecumenism between the historic Latin American churches, including of course the Roman Catholic Church. While there is no doubt that relationships with the Roman Catholic Church are to be continued, neither the basis nor the objectives of these relationships are clear. Alongside this is an emphasis on ecumenism which aims at overcoming denominationalism among the historic Protestant churches and strengthening relationships with Evangelical and Pentecostal churches. Third, especially in Brazil but also else-where, there are strong pleas for intercultural and interre-ligious ecumenism ("macro-ecumenism"). Throughout the continent this challenge arises especially in relationship to indigenous populations. These three perspectives cannot be easily reconciled.

I saw quite a different picture during a regional ecumeni-cal consultation with church leaders from the Pacific. It was obvious that "churchly ecumenism" finds little resonance in the Pacific, where most WCC member churches come from either Anglican, Methodist or Presbyterian-Congregational-ist background. There is widespread agreement that denomi-nationalism divides whereas culture unites. This understand-ing of the church in terms of denominational structures rather than in terms of a living community has consequences for the self-understanding of national councils of churches, which see themselves as closer to the cultural and social realities of these island nations. In some instances denominational pat-terns of hierarchy and leadership are legitimated against the background of indigenous concepts of authority represented through the system of chiefs. Ultimately, the concern for the future of ecumenism leads back to the basic question: what does it mean to be the church today?

Yet another type of ecumenical ambiguity is evident in Aotearoa New Zealand. In the mid-1980s, what was then the National Council of Churches in New Zealand under-went a transformation. There were several reasons for this: the growing sense of the country as "bicultural", recogni-tion of the separate existence of the Maori Council of Churches and the need to prepare for the entry into the Council of the Roman Catholic Church. The result was a new, much lighter ecumenical structure, intended to be open to wider community initiatives. But ecumenical com-mitment among the mainline churches has not been streng-thened in the process; rather, two profiles of ecumenism have emerged sharply. One focuses on integration with social movements in civil society, the other on the tradi-tional interchurch agenda, in particular, issues of faith and order. This has pulled the new ecumenical body into conflicting directions.

These three examples could be supplemented by many others. But even these brief summaries are enough to show the need for a clarification of the understanding of ecumenism. This task is made more urgent by the issues raised through Roman Catholic membership of councils of churches. For the Roman Catholic Church, as represented by the magisterium and underlined in the recent encyclical of Pope John Paul II *Ut unum sint*, the heart of ecumenism, to which all other dimensions are subsidiary, is the restoration of the visible unity of the church; and its understanding of what this is and of what is required to reach it is set forth in very clear terms. In many countries, particularly those with a strong Catholic majority, it claims the right to define the purpose of ecumenism and presents itself as the true leader of the ecumenical movement. This often creates embarrassment for the member churches of the World Council of Churches, who feel committed to the conciliar and dialogical understanding of church unity that has emerged over decades of ecumenical discussion.

Can the churches and those responsible for ecumenical organizations agree on a sufficiently firm common base for the understanding of ecumenism? Does ecumenism in the proper sense relate only to the search for communion among the Christian churches, or should it be opened up to relations with other religious communities — as is frequently advocated in Asia? Should the ecumenical movement reach beyond the churches to make alliances with other groups in civil society? What is the proper relationship between the commitment to church unity and to social justice? Are common witness and evangelism more important than church unity?

At stake in these questions is the oneness or coherence of the ecumenical movement. Thus they are decisive for the future of the ecumenical movement. Even if no common response is possible at present, we need some guidelines to give us a common sense of purpose in the midst of our differences of understanding. In view of the profound generational change taking place today, the answers will have to be formulated together with young people, who will be the ones to assume ecumenical responsibility in the first decades of the new century — provided that they are sufficiently convinced about the purpose and direction of the ecumenical movement.

On the basis of my many visits to member churches, this seems to me to be a fundamental challenge posed to the World Council of Churches on the eve of the third millennium.

2. On the Eve of the Third Millennium

The world in which persons who are now in their twenties — those who will, as we have said, shape events in the first decades of the coming century — have grown up is radically different not only from the world their grandparents knew when they were young, but also from the world of their parents. In the South, the enthusiasm which animated the struggles for liberation from colonialism and the processes of nation-building is far removed from the experience of young people today. Young people are fascinated by the new possibilities opened up by the communications media and rapid transportation. In the more affluent parts of the world, many young people from families of even modest means have visited more countries than the wealthiest persons of their grandparents' generation dreamed of seeing during an entire lifetime. At the same time, many are sharply aware of the precarious state of the human environment, and are urging their parents to adopt a different style of life. They do not share the faith in technological progress and unlimited growth which characterized their parents' generation, for what they see on the horizon are diminishing opportunities for education, structural unemployment and jobless growth. They sense that they are caught up in an irreversible dynamic of change which seems to escape any control. While their parents have had to come to terms with the impact of secularization, many of them are rediscovering religion and are searching for meaning and a sense of coherence.

Our societies have yet to absorb the profound changes of this outgoing century. The prevailing political structures, cultural patterns and moral attitudes are ill-suited to the challenges of the 21st century. The most effective adaptations seem to have come in business and the economy, which have become the moving force and setter of trends for worldwide cooperation under the banner of "globalization". Innovations in communication technology have accelerated this development. As a result, the rules of economic efficiency have increasingly come to govern political, social and cultural priorities.

The need to be "competitive" in the global market is eroding the power of governments to direct and control the economy in the interest of the common good and eclipsing concern for human well-being and the preservation of creation alike. The concept of the welfare state, hailed as a major achievement of postwar European reconstruction, is under increasing challenge. Everywhere in the South, programmes of "structural adjustment" imposed by international financial institutions have obliged the dismantling of systems of social security.

Perceptive observers agree that the present course of human development cannot be sustained in the long run. Even without indulging in apocalyptic prophecies, we can recognize clearly that meeting the challenges of the new century will require a fundamental reorientation in the forms of human life. The changes required go beyond scientific, technological or structural innovations and reach into the spiritual and moral foundations of humanity.

There is no doubt that this process of transformation, which will continue into the 21st century, is of decisive importance for the ecumenical movement. In many ways, this movement can be seen as the common effort of the Christian churches, inspired by the rediscovery of the vision of God's *oikoumene*, to overcome their defensive parochialism of earlier centuries and to come to terms with the conditions of the modern world. If the ecumenical movement is to regain its vitality — and in its present situation of uncertainty and stagnation it is easy to lose sight of how exciting and vital it has been — it will have to find a new vision which can inspire the young generation of today.

Three central challenges

The search for a new ecumenical vision must begin by identifying the characteristic features of the present process of transformation and discerning the challenges arising from them which call the churches to reassess their mission. Of course, the three challenges I shall mention here represent only one reading of the contemporary situation; and it is of the essence of the ecumenical movement to subject all such perceptions to dialogue and mutual questioning in order to arrive at a deeper understanding of the context in which the churches are called to fulfill together their common calling.

1. A life-centred vision

A decisive insight coming out of ecumenical work during the past quarter century has been a rediscovery and reaffirmation of the original scope of the Greek word *oikoumene* as "the whole inhabited earth". As global interdependence — and awareness of it in the churches — have increased since the 1960s, a wide-ranging discussion has arisen in the ecumenical movement over the relationship between the unity of the church and the unity of humankind. More recently, it has become ever clearer that this perspective on "the whole inhabited earth", based on a traditional human-centred view of the world and of history, is still too limited. One major challenge facing the ecumenical movement is thus the need to develop a life-centred understanding of the *oikoumene* which embraces all of God's creation.

Overcoming the human-centred view of the world and of history and recapturing the life-centredness at the heart of most religious traditions, including that of the Bible, takes us to the roots of our understanding of God, world and humanity, of our spirituality and our ethical norms. Widening our understanding of the *oikoumene* in this way also broadens our idea of the mission of the Christian community, inviting us to open our ecumenical explorations to the insights which other cultures and religious traditions can contribute to the search for a life-centred spirituality and ethic. Life-centredness requires us to learn a relationship of caring for all living beings and for all processes which sustain life. Human needs will have to be brought into a new balance with the needs and capabilities for regenerating life through the natural life-cycles. Human history will have to be reassessed as an important but limited part of the history of nature.

The call for a shift from a human-centred to a life-centred understanding has come along with a growing awareness of the ecological threats to human survival. We have become more conscious of how human life depends on the regenerating power of the natural life-cycles. The human habitat is not self-contained. Assuring its security over against the disruptive forces of nature is intertwined with the need to protect nature from the destructive interventions of human activity. The essential factors which sustain human life are water, arable land, climate, energy resources and the capacity of natural species to adapt to changing conditions. In all these areas, the dominant industrial mode of production and the growth-oriented patterns of the economy and of consumption have led to serious disturbances in the ecosphere, bringing the risk of rapidly increasing catastrophic developments. The consequences of accelerated climate change and the growing scarcity of drinkable water are only two examples of what lies ahead. Since the first United Nations conference on the environment in Stockholm and the first report of the Club of Rome, a clear change of consciousness has begun to take place, but the processes of decision-making are still totally inadequate to meet the growing challenge.

Increasingly we are coming to recognize that the ecumenical movement, whose dominant impetus has been that of Western Protestant Christianity, shares in the long-term consequences of the European Enlightenment. One important feature of this tradition has been the separation of the human person and the human community from their setting in the natural environment. Nature has been seen as a resource to be used and exploited for the benefit of the human community, something to be transformed into human culture. This inclination has been fortified by an interpretation of the doctrine of creation which sees humanity placed in the centre of God's creation with a mandate to subdue and rule over the earth. Today this understanding is being challenged as a one-sided interpretation of the biblical tradition. Especially through the influence of the worldview of the Orthodox churches, a more holistic ecumenical understanding of the human presence in God's creation has begun to emerge. But there can be no doubt of the human-centred foundations of the dominant Western culture and its influence on the understanding of the *oikoumene*.

2. *The acknowledgment of plurality*

A second significant shift in the understanding of the *oikoumene* is related to the fading dream of Christian hegemony and the growing challenge to acknowledge cultural and religious plurality as enduring features of human society.

This shift is one of the manifestations of a far wider process of cultural transformation. Struggles among human groups for cultural, religious, social and political predominance have shaped much of recorded human history. These struggles were extended and intensified by the emergence of the state and of the imperial form of political rule. One of the most dramatic examples of this, affecting large parts of the earth, was European colonialism, beginning with the conquest of Latin America five hundred years ago. The second half of the 20th century was characterized by another struggle for dominance: that between the two super-powers during the period of the so-called cold war. When the collapse of state socialism and the disappearance of the Soviet Union unexpectedly brought this rivalry to an end, some analysts even spoke of the "end of history", suggesting that the Western social and cultural pattern had definitively established its hegemony. Others now predict that the end of the cold war will lead to a new struggle for cultural and political dominance, characterized by a "clash of civilizations".

While both of these analyses remain in the framework of 20th-century political realism, the real challenge ahead is to transform the pattern of competition for hegemony into a new acknowledgment of plurality. Awareness of this plurality — of religions, of cultures, of ethnic and racial identities, of languages and of histories — has dramatically increased as the different parts of the earth have become interdependent. To be sure, the spread of Western civilization to all parts of the world has produced a certain homogenization of life-styles and cultural forms. But at the same time, efforts to defend and reaffirm indigenous cultures, religious traditions, ethnic and racial identities have increased. The semblance of a unified culture created by the worldwide network of electronic communication is in fact less and less connected with the everyday world of the vast majority of people.

Changes in the religious situation around the world are a crucial element in the transition to the 21st century. Contrary to expectations that secularism would continue to spread and further marginalize religion into the private sphere, we see religion reasserting itself in the public realm. Where this is expressed forcefully, it is often described in terms of religious fundamentalism. Whether or not this term is an appropriate one, it is clear that many expressions of the phenomenon to which it points can be interpreted as a form of collective resistance against claims to cultural hegemony. The question they pose is whether a sustainable form of living with religious plurality can be found. Naturally, this is a particular concern for the ecumenical movement; regrettably, under the influence of the fundamental distinction between religion and the Christian faith, most of Christian theology has unlearned the language of religious symbolism and thus finds it very difficult to respond to the new religious situation.

Obviously, there is no way back to the pre-modern situation in which self-contained, homogeneous communities shared the same ethnic origin, language, culture, values, religion and the like. The interdependence of human communities is here to stay, as are exposure to and interpenetration of different cultures and traditions due to increased mobility. Humanity has no choice but to develop ways of acknowledging cultural and religious plurality as a permanent social fact and to move from antagonistic competitiveness to communicative cooperation. Again, this challenges the "parochial" shape of human consciousness and of moral conscience, in which much of how we look at society and morality is rooted in the distinction between "ourselves" and "the others".

How can we learn to accept "the others" in their difference, not as a threat, but as a potential enrichment? This is a particularly pertinent question for the ecumenical movement, because the exclusivism of parochial consciousness grows to a large extent out of religious beliefs, including Christianity. Like all religions today, Christianity is challenged to reassess its long-standing exclusivist claims and to contribute to building a new culture which values and sustains plurality.

A key element of an ecumenical vision for the 21st century must be the search for ways in which Christian communities, in dialogue with people of other religious traditions, can develop forms of communication and standards of moral orientation which will make social, cultural and religious plurality sustainable rather than self-destructive.

3. The phenomenon of globalization

The early ecumenical movement emerged together with the spirit of *internationalism* as it was expressed in the establishment of the League of Nations. Indeed, one of the central documents from this pioneering period — the encyclical letter of the Ecumenical Patriarch in 1920 addressed to all churches everywhere — explicitly drew an analogy with the League of Nations in its call for a worldwide "*koinonia* of churches". Over the subsequent decades, the ecumenical movement has consistently supported, in words and actions, the search for a viable international social, economic and political order. It has called on churches to uphold the vision articulated in the Charter of the United Nations, and the World Council of Churches has collaborated with UN agencies in such areas as human rights and religious freedom, health and service to refugees.

The phenomenon we are witnessing at the end of this century is something quite different from the search for viable forms of international order: a *globalization* of human society, particularly in the areas of economy, finance and communication. Fostered and symbolized by interconnected networks of high-speed electronic communication, this globalization is beginning to transform all traditional ways of organizing society, exercising power and producing goods and services.

The systems of communication which create the possibility of globalization have brought some impressive achievements. Increasing access to and instantaneous transfer of information have expanded many people's knowledge and broadened their horizons, particularly with the steadily decreasing costs of computer capabilities. Churches and ecumenical organizations have only begun to take advantage of the potential of rapid communication worldwide and to incorporate this into their own processes of decision-making. Electronic transfer of information has sometimes been instrumental in curtailing the power of those who depend on ignorance and secrecy to maintain their control over others. The dream of "one world" — an image which has also fired the imagination of the ecumenical movement (and was in fact the title of a magazine published by the WCC from the mid-1970s to the mid-1990s) — seems to be on its way to becoming a reality.

But impressive as the achievements of globalization are, there are also abundant indicators of its internal contradictions. Increasing numbers of people are being excluded from the "one world" of this integrated system, condemned to mere survival on its fringes. Globalization symbolizes a form of human power which can no longer be controlled. Because the global economic and financial system recognizes no limits — whether of national boundaries, political sovereignty or ecological sustainability — it finally becomes self-destructive. Using biblical language, one might call this attempt to construct global unity a modern version of the tower of Babel, claiming for humanity the ability to manage the earth as an integrated whole, and thus abolishing the distinction between Creator and creation. To regard the earth as an integrated whole is the perspective of God; and it is a perspective into which human beings enter only in the attitude of prayer and adoration. Humanity is part of God's creation. It is placed within the limits of finitude, ultimately the limits of death. The potentially self-destructive dynamics of the process of globalization can be met only if human beings, individually and collectively, learn again to live within limits.

An ecumenical vision for the 21st century will have to confront this ambiguous version of human "oneness". It will have to rediscover the *oikoumene* as "God's household" (an image we shall look at more closely in the next chapter) — the space for life in relationships. The present trend towards globalization will have to be transformed by recovering a sense of sustainable limits for human existence.

Most of the fundamental ethical codes of the great religions are rooted in the insight that human life in community and in relationship with nature can be sustained only on the basis of an intentional self-limitation of power and greed. The recognition of people's minimum basic needs must be accompanied by an acknowledgment of the maximum gratification of desires which can be tolerated before greed and the excessive concentration of power lead to ruin. This acknowledgment of limits is based on an understanding of human existence as "being in relationship". Each human person is a centre of relationships. Our identity is formed through our relationships with other human beings, with our natural environment and ultimately with God. From the perspective of the Christian confession of the Trinity, God is understood as the ultimate centre of relationships. Living in relationships means acknowledging that "the other" sets limits on my freedom, power, need and security. Since "the other" is himself or herself a centre of relationships, our common task is to shape these relationships which constitute our identity into communicative and mutually supportive links.

Approaching the present trend towards globalization from this standpoint means re-evaluating the existing structures for organizing human life and activity according to the criterion of how well they can generate and sustain the vital relationships on which human life and survival depend. Both hierarchical structures of control and competitive systems of establishing and accumulating political and economic power pose a constant threat to the maintenance of this network of vital relationships. They must be replaced by participatory and decentralized forms of social, economic and political organization which recognize that the claims arising from the everyday life of people have priority over the systemic demands of super-structures.

The increasing fragmentation which is the reverse side of the trend towards globalization underscores the primary task of Christian churches to further the process of reconstructing sustainable human communities. This is reflected in the growing ecumenical interest in developing and strengthening forms of civil society over against the existing political, social and economic structures. For centuries, the churches have organized their own life along the lines of the prevailing structures of the state — whether in its hierarchical or democratic form. More recently, churches have been organizing themselves according to the patterns of the business world. An ecumenical vision that can address the ambiguities of growing globalization in the 21st century will have to be one which challenges the churches to understand themselves as a vital part of civil society, and at the same time to transcend the potentially exclusive claims of culture, racial origin and ethnic loyalties.

Catholicity and conciliarity: the lessons of JPIC

During the 20th century, Christianity has become truly ecumenical. As the gospel has been carried to the "ends of the earth", the centre of Christianity has shifted from Europe and North America to the southern hemisphere, not only in terms of numbers but also in terms of the vitality of Christian community life. The pre-eminence of the historic Christian traditions in which the ecumenical movement originated and which gave it its institutional forms is now being challenged by new expressions of the Christian faith, life and witness which are shaped by the interaction with other cultures and religious traditions. Pentecostalism is emerging as the dominant form of Protestant Christianity in Latin America, and in

Africa the growth of Independent or African-instituted churches is continuing.

But while the number of Christians worldwide has
increased along with the earth's population, the percentage
of Christian believers in comparison with people of other
faiths has not significantly changed. This is especially the
case in Asia, where half of humankind lives. Except for
South Korea and the Philippines, Christians continue to form
a very small minority in Asian countries. Despite sustained
efforts for evangelism and church growth, Christianity is
likely to remain a minority among other religious minorities.
Given the challenges of the transition into the 21st century
we have identified above, it will therefore be decisive for the
churches to manifest in their relationships the particular form
of universality which is rooted in the Christian faith.

The traditional term for this distinctive Christian understanding of universality is "catholicity". Neither a form of
globalization nor a mere acquiescence in plurality, catholicity is based on the recognition that the fullness of God's
presence is to be experienced in each local community which
gathers in the name of Christ and which recognizes its
essential and unbreakable relationship with all other such
local communities. The tension between the local church and
the universal church must be transformed into a relational
understanding of a worldwide church with its foundation in
the local communities assembled in each place. The ecumenical character and commitment of each local community is
then measured by how far it is prepared to recognize its
indissoluble relationship with all other communities as members of the worldwide body of Christ. This relationship is
acknowledged not only in mutual support and solidarity, but
also in recognizing differences and accepting mutual accountability to one another.

The early church worked out this relationship by
developing forms of *conciliar* life, first at the local, then at
ever-wider levels. Although conciliarity was later co-opted
for the purposes of the imperial *oikoumene*, it nevertheless
represented the most effective form of resistance to the

version of globalization represented by the Roman empire, for it affirmed the church as a community or *koinonia* in relationship with the Triune God.

If Christian ecumenism were understood as the practice of conciliar forms of life, it could become one of the most important counter-forces to the destructive effects of the globalization of contemporary culture. But the 20th-century ecumenical movement has not developed its institutional forms along these lines. Instead, international ecumenical institutions have followed the patterns of secular international cooperation in politics and society. It is the ethos of liberal Protestantism, with its affirmation of democratic forms of representation, participation and decision-making, which has shaped the World Council of Churches and other ecumenical bodies that have modelled themselves accordingly. The limitations of this framework for ensuring good governance and protecting and strengthening the fabric of vital relationships over against the tendencies of fragmentation and individualism are becoming apparent on all levels of social and political organization.

The ecumenical rediscovery in the 1970s of conciliarity and the conciliar form of life in the early church, largely due to the influence of the Orthodox churches, touched off a lively discussion of the theological and ecclesiological significance of conciliarity for the unity of the church. But the potential contribution of this rediscovery to developing appropriate forms of relationships among the churches and in the ecumenical movement has not really been explored. Could the tradition of conciliarity show the way to viable forms of ecumenical organization which are free from political institutionalization? The successes and failures of the so-called "conciliar process" for Justice, Peace and the Integrity of Creation (JPIC), initiated by the sixth assembly of the World Council of Churches (Vancouver 1983), may shed some light on this question.

The JPIC process may be seen as the product of the influence of social movements within the churches and a growing awareness of the dangers inherent in the process of progressive globalization. Its immediate origins lay in the passionate concern in Europe and North America about nuclear disarmament and the nuclear arms race. The peace movement opened up a debate which unleashed hitherto unsuspected forces of protest in society and in the churches.

As far as ecumenical social thought is concerned, the distinctive contributions of the JPIC process were (1) the identification of war and violence, hunger and poverty, and destruction of the natural environment as *interrelated life-destroying forces*; and (2) the intention to mobilize the churches as a whole to call the world to *repentance through confession and resistance*. In this, the JPIC process built on the experience of churches and Christian groups in mobilizing for the struggle against racism and apartheid and on the example of churches which had called for rejection of "the spirit, logic and practice" of deterrence as a strategy for defence against the threat of nuclear weapons.

The model of "conciliar" decisions to express the urgent call for an authoritative witness by the churches was inspired by the conciliar tradition of the ancient church (evoked by Dietrich Bonhoeffer already in 1934) and by the earlier WCC studies of councils and conciliarity. The action of the Vancouver assembly thus reflected a hope that the churches were ready to engage in a binding process of consultation and enter into fundamental commitments regarding justice, peace and the integrity of creation. To this was added the model of "covenanting before God and with one another", which picked up a tradition that had played an important role in the origins of civil society in the United States.

But problems soon emerged when it came to implementing the recommendation of the Vancouver assembly to engage the churches "in a conciliar process of mutual commitment (covenant) to justice, peace and the integrity of creation". In churches with a strong institutional and public structure, as in Germany, the idea that fired people's imagination was the proposal for a "peace council" which could speak authoritatively for the churches on issues of human survival. Although it was quickly evident that neither the

Orthodox nor the Roman Catholic churches would be prepared to accept the authority of such a peace council, many people continued to judge the conciliar process on the basis of their expectations of a peace council.

Others were most excited by the prospect of mobilizing all parts of the people of God. The model of covenant — taken up visibly at the Vancouver assembly itself in the form of a public commitment between assembly delegates from the USA and from Central America — was linked with the expectation that the conciliar process would lead to clear commitments obliging the churches to identify with the will of God's people and so to bring pressure to bear on the political process. The model here was the efforts of movements for social and political change.

Still others were primarily interested in clarifying new ethical challenges and guidelines arising from the inherent connection that was affirmed between justice, peace and the integrity of creation.

All of the various gatherings held as part of the conciliar process in Germany, the 1989 European Ecumenical Assembly in Basel and the WCC's world convocation on JPIC in Seoul in 1990 reflected these different ways of interpreting the original proposal from Vancouver. Each of these meetings produced documents which included not only recommendations but also explicit commitments. Yet the subsequent reception of these decisions in the participating churches proved to be problematic. It was not possible to transpose a process begun at the level of civil society to the institutional level of decision-making in the churches. The shortcomings and unclarities regarding the ecclesiological assumptions that underlay the conciliar process from the outset became visible.

From the standpoint of the World Council of Churches, the most important outcome of the conciliar process was the ten affirmations formulated by the Seoul convocation:

1. that all exercise of power is accountable to God;
2. God's option for the poor;

3. the equal value of all races and peoples;
4. that male and female are created in the image of God;
5. that truth is at the foundation of a community of free people;
6. the peace of Jesus Christ;
7. the creation as beloved of God;
8. that the earth is the Lord's;
9. the dignity and commitment of the younger generation;
10. that human rights are given by God.

The nature of these affirmations, however, has significantly changed since they were made, because of the dramatic alteration of the global situation in the years since the Seoul convocation. The affirmations originally grew out of a consciousness of standing before a *kairos*, a moment of special significance demanding an urgent prophetic call to confession and resistance. This diagnosis is echoed in the refrain "Now is the time...", which runs through the message from the Seoul convocation. It had its roots in the nuclear confrontation between the two power blocs, whose unimaginably destructive consequences were ever increasing and whose fragile equilibrium was more and more threatened by the development and deployment of more sophisticated delivery and defence systems alike. The disappearance of this confrontation in subsequent years has substantially altered the situation.

Of course, we are still confronted by basic ethical issues. But it is much more difficult today to draw the lines between good and evil, life and death, in terms which imply the need to take a *confessional* stance. In the present situation, characterized by the disintegration of moral guidelines and the postmodern reduction of ethical convictions to the level of individual preferences, the primary task would seem rather to be that of reconstructing the basis of an ethical culture and restoring the basic moral fabric of society. This task is most obvious in the countries of Eastern Europe, in Africa and in

South and Central America, which now have to work out a new basis for society after a long period of totalitarian rule or military dictatorship.

Although this new orientation differs from the original approach of the conciliar process for JPIC, its basic elements can already be discerned in the ecumenical discussions that led up to the world convocation and in the texts of Seoul itself. Three years earlier, the WCC's world consultation on the "ecumenical sharing of resources", in El Escorial, Spain, spoke of the need for a new value system based on justice, peace and the integrity of creation. The documents from Seoul itself repeatedly refer to the need to contribute to building a new culture — a culture of dialogue and solidarity, of active nonviolence, of respect for the right to life of all living beings.

This idea became the starting point for the continuing work on the conciliar process for JPIC within the World Council of Churches. The original approach, appealing for confession and resistance to the life-threatening forces of violence, hunger and poverty and the destruction of the environment, has been transformed into the quest for a "theology of life"; and the ten affirmations from Seoul are now read as indicators of the basic conditions for a sustainable culture. Creating a culture demands an act of construction or reconstruction. The new challenge thus lies in going beyond a critical analysis of the values governing modern culture to develop ways of living which value being-in-relationship rather than acquisitiveness and competition. It is based on the insight that freedom, power, love, security and well-being can thrive only if they are shared.

Conciliarity and civil society

Introducing the idea of civil society into the ecumenical discussion of church and society may help to clarify some of the tensions surrounding the conciliar process. The concept of civil society draws attention to the autonomy and irreducible complexity of the world of everyday life. The logic or rationality according to which civil society operates is different from that of politics or economic life. Politics is concerned with acquiring, maintaining or increasing power, economic activity with accumulating capital through the process of competition. Civil society is about creating and preserving relationships and fostering communication in the widest sense. Its processes are concerned first and foremost with promoting the quality of life through reliable and meaningful relationships — not with exercising power or accumulating capital. Based on reciprocity and trust, they resist the logic of competition and rivalry.

All economic and political processes use and depend on a network of relationships in everyday life. But they cannot regenerate this network; indeed they can destroy it. In civil society, communication is not first and foremost instrumental or functional, but remains open. Transmitting information or creating consensus around a position or a demand are less important than exchange and interaction to strengthen and regenerate relationships. As opposed to economic or political activities, civil society is concerned with the realm of culture, not for the sake of political effectiveness or commercial value, but for building coherent relationships.

But civil society is not a closed system. The sustainability of any society depends on the interaction between the informal processes of civil society and the formal processes of politics and economics. Civil society forms the basis of political power and sets the limits to its legitimate exercise. Elementary rights or freedoms are intended to protect civil society from the encroachments of the logic of power. If the political process respects this borderline, the civil society is reinforced and political rule is legitimated. While all power uses some means of coercion to impose itself, coercion and violence are directly contrary to the rationality of civil society. Political power earns and confirms its legitimacy precisely by the self-limitation of keeping the sphere of civil society free from the use of violence and from structures of discrimination that infringe on the freedom and dignity of the citizens. The system of representative democracy based on elections presupposes the existence of an effectively functioning civil society and an active basis of trust in the social order. Where political parties claim a monopoly on the legitimation of political power or the institutions of civil society are structured according to party political representation, civil society is suffocated.

Similarly, civil society is the basis and precondition of an effectively functioning economy in the context of the market. The satisfaction of basic needs and the right to participate in society and the economy must be guaranteed in the realm of civil society. This is a matter of the common good, and must not be governed by private interests. Cooperative forms of economic activity transpose the model of the large household or extended family to the basic sector of formal economic processes. Its characteristics are communal or cooperative production; sharing of resources and benefits, means and abilities; solidarity in covering risks and deliberate refusal to calculate payments and counter-payments of any kind; and confidence that these will balance out in the long run. We find these basic forms of economic activity, rooted in the principle of good faith, in mutual assistance among neighbours and voluntary community work. The present trend to subject all this — including the securing of the basic means of existence — to the market rules of supply and demand and individual profit undermines the basis on which every formal economy is built. This is indirectly confirmed by the growing importance of the so-called "informal sector" cropping up in many national economies.

Civil society is an analytical concept intended to help us to sharpen our perception of social reality. The term should not be used in a descriptive sense; even less should it be idealized or romanticized and used prescriptively. This analytical perspective can in fact help us to discern more clearly the opportunities and limits of the conciliar process for JPIC, which clearly operated on the borderline line between civil society and the formal political and economic structures.

In retrospect, it is clear that whenever political influence and pressure must be brought to bear, the open processes of conciliar communication, which allow for controversy and encourage debate, have to be curtailed in order to suit the needs of formulating common statements and addressing common demands to decision-makers in church or society. In order to mobilize social and political power, the conciliar process was thus subjected to a political rationality.

Confession and resistance are political as well as spiritual acts; that is, they are intended to be publicly effective. If the political structures have forfeited their legitimacy, it may be necessary to extend a process within civil society into the field of politics in order to mobilize political pressure. The last phase of the struggle against the apartheid regime in South Africa exemplified this. Public prayer for the collapse of illegitimate tyrannical rule is an extreme act of conciliarity. The case of South Africa also shows how important it is for churches, once legitimate political structures have been put in place, to concentrate on re-establishing the autonomy of their internal processes and safeguarding their independence from the pressures of political rationality.

The dialectic between the logic of politics and the logic of civil society can also be observed in the development of conciliar forms in the life of the churches. Conciliarity can be understood as the practice and discipline of fellowship. Since fellowship or *koinonia* embraces both participation and sharing, it can be seen as a kind of Christian counterpart to civil society. Conciliarity did not take the extraordinary form of a universal council until the 4th century — and when it did, this was largely the result of political intervention in the sphere of the church. For the sake of the unity of the empire, it was thought necessary to conclude the open conciliar process of consultation with authoritative decisions which were then to be enforced by imperial law.

The conciliar process for JPIC focussed on mobilizing resistance and producing binding commitments or authoritative acts of confession because of what I called earlier a "*kairos* diagnosis", a conviction that it was necessary to withdraw legitimacy from the global political and economic system in order to preserve the world from self-destruction.

The plausibility of this diagnosis was controversial from the start — which explains the limited effectiveness of the conciliar process and of its various declarations. The subsequent changes in the global situation have necessitated a fundamental reappraisal of such an antagonistic view of social relations. Surely the question of the legitimacy of global political and economic structures must continue to be debated, but not solely in terms of changing the system. The aim must rather be to rebuild and restore vital relationships within civil society.

For this reason, it seems urgent to return to the basic forms of conciliarity by strengthening the capacity for reciprocity, solidarity, dialogue and nonviolent resolution of conflicts and reinforcing the processes of sharing. The main emphasis should be on contributing to transformation on the level of systems by changing the cultural consciousness. The biblical concept of *metanoia* — in the sense of conversion or a change of heart — points in this direction. Such conversion is not a momentary act of moral decision, but a process of learning and a new way of living.

This explains why the continuing ecumenical discussion of the conciliar process for JPIC has focussed on a "theology of life". "Life" and "culture" are pointers to the realm of experience most appropriately analyzed with the help of the concept of "civil society". If, as I have suggested, the form which the processes of civil society take in the sphere of the church is conciliarity, then the ecumenical movement as a whole can be interpreted as an endeavour to strengthen the dimension of civil society within the larger institutional structure of the church. While the ecumenical movement has always been concerned with processes of renewing the church from within, the revitalization of conciliar forms in the life of the churches and in their ecumenical relationships can introduce a decisive perspective into the search for viable forms of organizing human community.

All relationships within civil society are based on a sense of moral obligation and a basic trust in the reliability of the social order. Under the impact of aggressive globalization and the spread of materialistic values, this essential moral fabric is beginning to erode. The role of religion in all societies is to maintain and nurture the sense of basic trust and to keep alive a hope that transcends the prevailing conditions of life.

Conciliarity refers to the capacity of the Christian community to affirm relationships and to generate common symbols which are inclusive and promote coherence even in the presence of conflicts and differences. Conciliarity allows the churches to affirm the distinctive universality of the Christian faith over against the forces of globalization. Christian faith can entrust the responsibility for the coherence of the world as a whole to the eschatological design of God. Liberated from the unbearable burden of global responsibility, it can open the space for recognizing genuine and enduring differences of cultures and local contexts and resisting the claims of exclusivism and sectarianism. Reactivating conciliar forms of life and relationships and broadening their scope could thus be the decisive contribution of the ecumenical movement in facing the challenges of the 21st century.

3. Biblical Orientations for the Future

At the core of the three challenges identified in the previous chapter — shifting our worldview from human-centredness to life-centredness, coming to terms with plurality and developing the ability to live within limits — is the need to overcome the modern mindset of separating culture from nature, the individual from the community, mind from matter, subject from object, by rediscovering the relational structure of reality.

The modern mindset values linear processes of growth over cyclical processes of generation and re-generation. It shapes the dominant values of individualism and consumerism, competitiveness and accumulation, success and prosperity. By contrast, the ethical codes rooted in all the religious traditions of humanity proceed from the insight that human life in community and in relationship with the natural environment is sustainable only as long as there is an intentional self-limitation of power and greed.

Recognizing that this common ethical tradition of humanity, which has formed the moral fabric of cultures and societies, is beginning to erode, the "Declaration Towards a Global Ethic" adopted by the World Parliament of Religions in 1993 states categorically: "No new global order without a new global ethic" — that is, "a fundamental consensus on binding values, irrevocable standards and personal attitudes". Without this, "sooner or later every community will be threatened by chaos or dictatorship, and individuals will despair" (*A Global Ethic*, pp.18, 21).

The Catholic theologian Hans Küng, who drafted this Declaration, has himself used the Ten Commandments, the classic form of an ethic of self-limitation, as the basis for formulating "four irrevocable directives" or commitments at the core of a global ethic: a new culture of (1) nonviolence and respect for life, (2) solidarity and a just economic order, (3) tolerance and a life of truthfulness, (4) equal rights and partnership between men and women (pp.24ff.). The whole Declaration is a clarion call for a "transformation of consciousness", a "conversion of heart", especially among religious believers.

Our analysis of the conciliar process for Justice, Peace and the Integrity of Creation has pointed in the same direction. And the conversations I have had during my visits to WCC member churches with people in positions of political and social responsibility have confirmed that their central expectation of the churches today is that they will address the disintegration and fragmentation on all levels of human society and cooperate with others in rebuilding the moral fabric that sustains life in community. This is a task of basic "moral formation", of rediscovering and reappropriating the values which are at the core of the new cultural consciousness advocated by the Declaration Towards a Global Ethic.

Captivated by institutions?

Since cultural consciousness is shaped through interactions in civil society, the question of what it means to be the church today should therefore lead the churches to insert themselves more consciously into the life of civil society. For this task of rebuilding sustainable communities, the tradition of conciliarity, as we have seen, gives the churches a treasury of insights and a model of relationships.

What blocks many historic churches from drawing on this resource of conciliarity is the institutional captivity which they seem unable to break out of. This is not a new phenomenon. We alluded earlier to the fact that the traditional categories for understanding the church have largely been borrowed from the structure of political organization. Even the Greek and Hebrew words which are the equivalents to our concept of church were terms originally used for secular political concepts. Thus the episcopal and hierarchical image of the church corresponds to the monarchical form of government. The metropolitan and diocesan system of church administration was borrowed from the administrative structure of the Roman Empire. The conciliar form of universal church unity was the fruit of an imperial initiative.

The Protestant Reformation occurred during a period of gradual transition to the republican form of government. This has its clearest counterpart in the Presbyterian-Reformed tradition. Presbyterianism could be described as a kind of ecclesial aristocracy, which confers authority on elders and elected representatives as legitimate holders of ecclesial office, whereas the Lutheran tradition transferred the older imperial-monarchical type of government onto smaller territories. The so-called left wing of the Reformation, represented by Baptist and Congregationalist dissenters, gave priority to the freedom of the church from the state and freedom of conscience. This led to an increasing individualization of the reception of divine grace and a radical democratic understanding of the church as a voluntary association of believers. In the United States, the denominational system is based on the equality of believers and the equality of local churches and church associations. In this context the synodical form of participatory church government found its first clear expression.

More recent approaches such as liberation theology, black theology and feminist theology, drawing on biblical references to the Christian community as aliens and pilgrims who are scattered in this world but whose citizenship is in heaven, have rediscovered the church as a "contrast society". This image of the church as an alternative community, kept alive throughout church history in monastic and reform movements, has also been reactivated in contemporary discipleship groups, house churches and voluntary communities. Rooted in the recognition of a clear distinction between the church and the dominant society, the memory of this alternative image is in fact one of the origins of the basic democratic differentiation between civil society and the state or government.

The recognition of institutionalism as one of the "nontheological factors" which hamper genuine ecumenical relationships among the churches and prevent them from manifesting their catholicity goes back to early ecumenical discussions. Although the process of de-institutionalization is painful, there is no other path to a genuine ecumenical renewal of the churches today. This is especially true, perhaps, for those institutional expressions of Protestant denominationalism which have adapted themselves more and more to the management model of the modern business corporation, separating themselves them even further from the everyday life of the people in civil society.

But this call does not come only to the churches. De-institutionalization is also required of ecumenical organizations. Even if many of these go by the name "council", their ethos and institutional structures are shaped less by the spirit of genuine conciliarity than by the rules of representative democracy. A typical preoccupation in these organizations is for "ownership", control and power (the logic of the political system) rather than for communication and relationships (the logic of civil society).

For this reason, relationships between churches and Christian communities on the local and national levels are a test case for the viability of ecumenical structures. In the local setting, few of the issues dividing the churches or threatening their relationships run along denominational or confessional lines. This is especially true of the pressing ethical concerns about life and death, procreation and birth control, genetic engineering, sexual orientation, violence against women and children, racism and all other forms of discrimination. The criterion for reassessing the institutional structures of ecumenical organizations must be this: are their activities and the way they function geared to building and nurturing the kind of relationships between the churches which enable the common life and witness of local Christian communities as communities of hope?

The promise of koinonia

To reaffirm the relational character of the church as a community of people reflects a different emphasis from that of traditional ecumenical discussions about ecclesiology. These have been dominated by efforts to reach a common understanding of the "nature of the church" or to bridge the gaps between the episcopal, presbyterian and congregationalist forms of church order, ministry and decision-making. These inherited differences come particularly to the fore in church union negotiations — since it is in its structured order that the church expresses its identity — thus usually leaving the task of building up new communities at the local level until after the inauguration of the united church.

Yet the classic statement on unity by the WCC's third assembly (New Delhi 1961) already spoke of the unity of the church as a process in which people "are brought by the Holy Spirit into one fully committed fellowship". The commentary to the statement goes on to explain:

> The word "fellowship" (*koinonia*) has been chosen because it describes what the church truly is. "Fellowship" clearly implies that the church is not merely an institution or organization. It is a fellowship of those who are called together by the Holy Spirit and in baptism confess Christ as Lord and Saviour. They are thus "fully committed" to him and to one another. Such a fellowship means for those who participate in it nothing less than a renewed mind and spirit, a full participation in common praise and prayer, the shared realities of penitence and forgiveness, mutuality in suffering and joy, listening together to the same gospel, responding in faith, obedience and service, joining in the one mission of Christ in the world, a self-forgetting love for all for whom Christ died, and the reconciling grace which breaks down every wall of race, colour, caste, tribe, sex, class and nation. Neither does this "fellowship" imply a rigid uniformity of structure, organization or government. A lively variety marks corporate life in the one Body of one Spirit (*New Delhi Report*, pp.119f.).

This idea of the church as a community of people, living in "fully committed fellowship" among one another and rooted in the *koinonia* of the Triune God, has been at the centre of recent ecumenical dialogues on the understanding of the church. The statement on "The Unity of the Church as Koinonia: Gift and Calling" adopted by the WCC's seventh assembly (Canberra 1991) inspired the work of the fifth world conference on Faith and Order (Santiago de Compostela 1993), under the theme "Towards Koinonia in Faith, Life and Witness". Since then, the question of the understanding of the church as koinonia has become the central focus of efforts to formulate ecumenical perspectives on ecclesiology.

Interpreting the church as koinonia or community shifts attention from its features as a structured body to the relational character of its life. The doctrinal "marks of the church" are of secondary interest; what matters most is the quality of the fellowship the church manifests in its life as a community. The diversity of gifts present in that community becomes more important than its institutional ordering. Old controversies can then be approached in a new light. Baptism is understood as the acceptance of the new common identity in Christ, drawing women and men, masters and slaves, Greeks and Jews into an inclusive community (Gal. 3:28). Above and beyond theological discussions about the "real presence" and the understanding of Christ's self-sacrifice for us, the eucharist becomes the act in which sharing the broken bread and the cup nurtures the community and rebuilds it as a fellowship of shared life. This same relational perspective transforms the ecumenical discussions about ministry, which is seen as the service that is necessary to build up the community and maintain its inner unity as well as its relatedness to other local communities.

The materials from the world conference on Faith and Order in Santiago provide ample evidence of the fruitfulness of this new approach to the understanding of the church. Here I want to highlight three features which deserve particular attention.

1. Interpreting the church and its unity as koinonia first of all opens up new possibilities to appreciate continuing diversities and differences within the community and to come to terms with the experience of plurality. While it has always been affirmed ecumenically that unity does not mean uniformity in all aspects of doctrine and life of the church, the continuing concern about the "limits to diversity" suggests that diversity is being perceived as a potential threat to the life of the community. A relational understanding of the church as community opens our eyes to the fact that it is by the very diversity of its members' gifts and potentials that

any viable community lives. As long as the members in their diversity acknowledge their constitutive relatedness within the community, their differences sustain rather than threaten the unity. Thus the community of the church can be endangered not only by the sectarian defence of diversities and particularities but also by a kind of "fundamentalism" of unity. Continued deepening of the unity of the church will therefore have to focus on the task of deepening the relational quality of its life as a community of sharing, of participation, of mutual accountability and of learning.

2. A second element to be underlined concerns the place of the Christian community in the wider human community. The shift of focus we have noted in the ecumenical discussion of ecclesiology has been accompanied by a renewed interest in exploring the links between ecclesiology and ethics. In the course of this, the Christian community has been recognized afresh as the setting in which a continuous process of "moral formation" takes place. Ethics or morality is not primarily a matter of formulating norms on which to base ethical judgments. Rather, it is a process by which people learn in community the distinction between good and evil and how to walk the way towards a fully human life. Thus ethical wisdom is transmitted in stories, symbols, parables and examples rather than in authoritative teaching of rules.

The question of how the Christian community can become a setting in which successive generations appropriate the wisdom and knowledge of values and basic orientations for life is especially critical in those communities where the moral fabric which holds them together is disintegrating. A particularly burning challenge to the churches is the question of how they can help in the resolution of conflicts between ethnic communities, more and more of which seem to turn into violent confrontations. In an atmosphere of communalism and mutual exclusiveness, how can the Christian community protect its own integrity as an open community? How can it strengthen the readiness to accept and respect the otherness of the other? The Apostle Paul taught us to understand forgiveness and reconciliation as the inner source for the establishment of koinonia with God and of community among one another. The Christian community is called to become the place where the tension between the struggle for justice and the commitment to reconciliation is overcome in the effort to build viable and sustainable human communities.

3. A third key insight is the understanding of the koinonia of the church as a community on the way, engaged in an open pilgrimage. The pilgrimage of the Christian community is here understood as a continuous process of *metanoia* or conversion. Being in relationship means being prepared to expose oneself to the radical otherness of the other, to make oneself vulnerable, to be changed in one's own being by the process of encounter. It also means accepting the fears and anxieties that such encounters with genuine otherness arouse in us. It means accepting *kenosis*, a potential loss of identity and the pain of brokenness in our own communities and between our communities. In its pilgrimage, the church as a community shares in the way of Christ, which is the way into suffering and to the cross. This way of the suffering Messiah — rather than the model of the conquering Christ — must therefore also be the model for the mission of the church.

Salt and light

Among the most important biblical metaphors for understanding the mission of the Christian community today are the two images or short parables of the salt of the earth and the light of the world (Matt. 5:13-16). To understand these images we must note that Matthew's gospel places them directly after the Beatitudes. It is the community of the Beatitudes, that is, the community of the poor and persecuted, who are called the salt of the earth and the light of the world.

What did the evangelist's contemporaries, rooted in the language of the Hebrew Bible, hear when these images were used? In putting together these two parables, Matthew was drawing on Jewish tradition. In their teaching the rabbis used both salt and light as metaphors to explain the nature of the law as something vitally necessary for the life of the community of the covenant. Both were very precious and scarce. Salt could even be used as a currency. We can easily miss the profound symbolism which salt and light represented for earlier generations, for salt to us is an everyday commodity, relatively cheap and used for certain specific purposes; and we have become accustomed to the availability of light everywhere and at any time at the flip of a switch.

Ancient Jewish traditions linked salt with the act of liturgical sacrifice. "With all your offerings you shall offer salt" (Lev. 2:13). Salt was used to consecrate a covenant, an act of fellowship (cf. the "covenant of salt" in Num. 18:19, or the "salt of the covenant" in Lev. 2:13). In the New Testament, the version of the parable about salt in Mark's gospel adds the following sentence: "Have salt in yourselves, and be at peace with one another" (Mark 9:50; some manuscripts put it even more directly: "Have the *salt of fellowship*..."). At the opening of the Acts of the Apostles (Acts 1:4) is a sentence which literally means: "While he [Jesus] *shared salt* with them, he ordered them not to leave Jerusalem."

What emerges from these references is that salt in the context of the liturgy of sacrifice gave symbolic expression to that which binds into covenantal fellowship. Beyond this highly symbolic level of meaning are more familiar images based on the use of salt as a means to purify (Ex. 30:35), to preserve (2 Kings 2:20ff.) or to give flavour to food (Job 6:6). All these different shades of meaning may have been present in the ears of the first readers and hearers of Matthew's gospel. To call this small community "salt of the earth" was to identify them as the consecrating link of the covenant, as that which purifies, preserves and sanctifies the earth, that is, renders it holy and acceptable before God.

It is not easy for us to penetrate into this symbolic language. We think of salt as something meant to be dissolved in food in order to give it some basic flavour. Thus if we read this little parable with modern eyes, we might even be tempted to see it as an argument for dissolving the identity of the Christian community in order to give the wider human community some flavour. Such a reading would entirely miss the setting of the readers for whom the gospel of Matthew was written, who could never have imagined such a generalized "culture Christianity". Furthermore, it would miss the very point Matthew is making, for the words "but if salt has lost its taste, how can its saltiness to be restored?" can be read as an explicit warning against the dissolving of the salt. The saltiness of the salt must be preserved.

The imagery here is — perhaps deliberately — paradoxical. The thrust of the parable is to encourage the small community: "Retain in yourselves the quality of salt. Be active like salt! For it is that which humanity and the earth need for life. Salt can only be salt; therefore, accept the fact of being salt. Do not fear the consequences, such as persecution, for it is only when salt stops acting as salt that it will be thrown away to be trampled underfoot."

What is at stake here is the role of the Christian community in and for the world. It can assume this role only if it does not dissolve and disappear, but remains recognizable as salt, as that which consecrates the covenant of life and which preserves and purifies. Only a little salt is needed to accomplish this twofold task of consecrating and establishing the community of the covenant and of maintaining integrity by stopping the process of decay and disintegration. In the traditional vocabulary of the church these would be described as the "priestly" and the "prophetic" functions of the Christian community as salt of the earth. Each is vital for the integrity of the life of the world. The Christian community as "salt of the earth" is thus more than just the "religious component" in the general flavour of the culture. Its function is critical, even aggressive, in the sense of preventing disintegration, decay and rottenness; and it is positive in the sense of being a healing, purifying force which re-establishes the links of fellowship in the community.

The same double thrust reappears in the metaphor of light. Already in the preceding chapter Matthew has taken up the eschatological symbolism of light and darkness by quoting from Isaiah 9:2: "The people who sat in darkness have seen a great light, and for those who sat in the region and shadow of death, light has dawned" (Matt. 4:16). If we look further at the prophetic use of the light metaphor, we are reminded of the figure of the servant of God who is appointed to be "a covenant to the people, a light to the nations" (Isa. 42:6; cf. 49:6), as well as the image of the pilgrimage of the nations to Zion attracted by the brightness of God's light which will in the last days descend on his holy mountain and on the city of Jerusalem (cf. Isa. 60; Isa. 2:2f.; Micah 4).

If we incorporate this rich prophetic imagery into our hearing and reading of the light parable, its meaning becomes transparent. Just as Israel and the servant of God were to be light to the nations, so the community of the disciples of Christ is meant to be the light that shines for "*all* in the house", for all people. It is to live as an eschatological community, attracting people from afar by virtue of the glorious light of God which has been placed in its hands in the gospel of Christ. Therefore, the twofold message to the Christian community is similar to that of the salt parable: "Accept yourself as this light which is in and for the world. Do not allow fear or lack of faith to tempt you to hide your light. This light will shine and bring into the open what is being hidden. And when you allow this light of the gospel and this light of life shaped by the spirit of the gospel to shine forth, remember that you do so not in order to attract attention to your own community, but so that all might 'give glory to your Father in heaven' (Matt. 5:16)." This is the final point of both parables and at the same time a safeguard against Christian triumphalism. The Christian community is to be an icon, to become transparent so that the ultimate source of light and the integrity of life can shine through it.

As symbols, salt and light stand for the integrity and viability of life. The community of the disciples of Christ is entrusted with the message of the good news which brings life, restores, heals and illuminates, just as it brings out into the open what is hidden and secret and acts against decay and disintegration.

Salt and light, which are vital for life, constitute a threat to the forces of death, destruction and oppression. A community which lives as salt of the earth and light of the world will share in this predicament. Just like its master, it will be perceived as threatening by those who draw their power from secrecy and their profit from spoiling the very sources of life.

The household of life

A key ecumenical insight, affirmed emphatically at the time of the WCC's fourth assembly (Uppsala 1968), is that the scope of the *oikoumene* goes beyond the community of Christian churches to embrace the whole human community. In the course of ecumenical discussions in the 1970s, however, controversy arose over this "secular" understanding of the *oikoumene*. As a consequence, the term "ecumenical" and its derivatives are again understood generally to refer only to matters of concern between Christian churches. One might argue that this limitation of the meaning of the term corresponds to the historical fact that the "ecumenical movement" has been a development rooted in and involving the Christian churches. But if this is taken to imply that ecumenism is church-centred in the sense of being largely separated from human concerns in society, economics and politics, then it is imperative to recapture the wider notion of the *oikoumene* and of the ecumenical calling of the churches in the world. And, as mentioned earlier, our new awareness of the ecological threat obliges us to transcend even the *oikoumene* of the inhabited human world to recognize that God's *oikoumene* embraces all of God's creation.

Here another biblical image may help to widen and clarify our understanding of ecumenism. This is an image related to the root word from which *oikoumene* is derived in Greek — *oikos*, meaning "house" or "household". All of God's creation is meant to be a house or household to be inhabited by all living beings. It is to be cared for and kept inhabitable for the generations to come. Our understanding of the *oikoumene* must overcome its human-centred character and recover the biblical understanding that all of life is relational and interdependent and sustained by the power of God's Spirit, who is confessed in the creed as the "Giver of Life". I would thus propose an interpretation of *oikoumene* as the "one household of life" and of our task as discerning the rules of living together in peace and wholeness as members of this one household where God through the Spirit dwells among God's people (Eph. 2:19-22).

The first letter of Peter and the letter to the Ephesians develop this metaphor of the house or household into a comprehensive symbol for the *oikoumene* which reaches beyond the relationships in the Christian and the human community and culminates in the revelation of the mystery of God's will in Christ "as a plan for the fullness of time to gather up all things in him, things in heaven and things on earth" (Eph. 1:10). It was in fact Philip Potter's masterly exposition of the "house of living stones" (1 Pet. 2:4ff.) in his address to the WCC's Vancouver assembly in 1983 which stimulated my own effort in an earlier book — *Ecumenism in Transition* (German original 1989, English translation, Geneva, WCC Publications, 1991) — to dig more deeply into the rich biblical material which would support this choice of a key metaphor for a new ecumenical vision, a metaphor which expresses the interrelatedness of all life and helps to unfold the notion of koinonia/communion in both its vertical and horizontal dimensions (cf. esp. ch. 4, pp.79ff.). Here I want to emphasize that this metaphor can also serve to liberate our thinking about the church as a social reality from its traditional dependency on symbolism drawn from political or economic life.

This image can open our minds to the wealth of symbolism hidden in the parables of Jesus, which use language drawn from the everyday interchange between human existence in community and the processes of life in creation. Besides salt and light, which we looked at above, the metaphors of the leaven, the mustard seed and the grain which must die in order to bear fruit come to mind. With specific reference to the household, the "round table" in the "open house", as an expression of neighbourliness among ordinary people and as a symbol of hospitality, of turning towards the other, becomes a mark of the Christian community as a "household" within civil society, which is itself dependent on the processes of sustenance and regeneration in the "one household of life".

The renewed interest in the Christian community as a space for moral formation calls attention to a feature of the *oikos* metaphor which deserves greater attention. The Apostle Paul in his letters refers to the process of building community with the term *oikodomé* (cf. Rom. 14:19; 15:2; 1 Cor. 14:5, 12, 26). Paul is interested not simply in the processes of forming a community in the traditional sense, but also in the building of a new moral "culture". The concept of *oikodomé* is thus directly linked with the quest for a new ethics of life in relationship. It aims at strengthening the church as a community of hope, solidarity and trust, in which the rules of a new life-centred culture and ethic can be learned and practised.

4. The Call to Conversion

The themes which have shaped the reflections of each of the WCC assemblies have always emerged from the context in which the delegates from all the member churches gather. For example, "Man's Disorder, God's Design" spoke eloquently of the sense of the churches as they came together in Amsterdam in 1948 to form the WCC, with memories of the devastation of the second world war and apprehensions about a new "cold" war uppermost in everyone's mind. "Behold, I Make All Things New" took the biblical words of Christ as the standpoint for responding to the spirit of innovation and change abroad in 1968 when the fourth assembly met in Uppsala. Against the powerful, death-dealing forces of injustice, war and environmental destruction, "Jesus Christ — the Life of the World", the theme of the sixth assembly (Vancouver 1983) was a powerful affirmation of faith and life.

The biblical jubilee

Already in the early stages of planning for the WCC's eighth assembly, the idea arose of linking its theme to the biblical tradition of the jubilee. The biblical jubilee, according to Leviticus 25, follows on the cycle of seven "sabbath years". The constitution of the World Council of Churches stipulates that assemblies, at which delegates from all member churches assess the work of the Council and set its policies for the coming period, should normally be held every seven years. The eighth assembly, taking place in the year of the WCC's fiftieth anniversary, therefore completes a cycle of seven assembly periods.

Beyond this symbolic analogy, the biblical and theological dimensions of the jubilee motif provide a fertile source of inspiration for a WCC assembly. The intention of the jubilee as set out in Leviticus 25 was periodically to break the inevitability of acquisitiveness and domination, which lead to exclusion, and to restore the opportunities for life in community to all. The jubilee year was to begin on the day of atonement, the occasion for reconciliation with God and among the people. It would be signalled by the sounding of the trumpet and the proclamation of "liberty throughout the land to all its inhabitants...; you shall return, every one of you, to your property and every one of you to your family" (Lev. 25:10). The central ordinance that all families be allowed to return to their ancestral land in the jubilee year was combined with the rules for the sabbath year: release of slaves, cancellation of debts and cessation of sowing and harvesting to allow the land a complete rest.

While we have no direct evidence that the jubilee year was ever actually observed, the way it is described in Leviticus 25 is nevertheless a forceful expression of the vision of a new beginning, a return to the order of community life instituted by the will of God. In the prophetic tradition (Isa. 61:1-2; Ezek. 46:17) the jubilee was understood as a symbol of salvation offered by God.

In his preaching Jesus appropriated the sabbath and jubilee tradition as a concrete representation of the coming kingdom of God, extending its promise even beyond the people of the covenant. In his first sermon at Nazareth (Luke 4:18ff.), Jesus proclaimed liberty by quoting from Isaiah 61 and concluding with the affirmation: "Today this scripture has been fulfilled in your hearing" (v.21). The sabbath-year rule regarding the cancellation of debts, which Leviticus 25 integrates into the jubilee framework, is reflected in the Lord's prayer (Matt. 6:12), which thus becomes a jubilee prayer: forgive us our debts as we forgive those who are indebted to us. The Greek word for forgiving used here is found in the Septuagint translation of both Leviticus 25:10 and Isaiah 61:1 as an equivalent of the Hebrew word for the "release" of captives and prisoners. The parable of the unfaithful servant (Matt. 18:23ff.) is a reminder that one reason for the loss of liberty in those days was precisely the failure to repay debts. A further echo of the jubilee message is found in 2 Corinthians 6:2: "See, now is the acceptable time; see, now is the day of salvation!" — which follows directly on the proclamation of reconciliation.

These reinterpretations transformed the Leviticus legislation into a powerful prophetic vision of new life in community in the horizon of the kingdom of God. Jesus and Paul radicalized the periodicity of the sabbath and the jubilee year, focusing instead on the eschatological *now* or *today*. God offers the jubilee of healing and restoring life, of forgiveness and liberation from bondage. *Any moment* can become the year of God's favour, the time of salvation. Now is therefore the time of liberation, remission, forgiveness, reconciliation. These affirmations have become central to the Christian understanding of the gospel of Jesus Christ.

Later Christian interpretation of the jubilee, however, has largely forgotten its concrete focus. This is particularly true of those sectors of the church which have grown quite comfortable with the way things are. Only recently have some biblical scholars rediscovered how deeply Jesus rooted his proclamation in the original jubilee tradition. Newer translations ("forgive us our *trespasses*, or *sins*") have tended to obscure the impossibility of praying the Lord's prayer without being confronted by the jubilee call to cancel all debts. Yet the jubilee principle of the restitution of land, cancellation of debts and liberation of slaves and captives (an element reflected in many African American spirituals) remains one of the powerful utopias in Jewish and Christian history, with a virtually inexhaustible potential for critically unmasking the status quo of domination and dependency and for sustaining visions of a transformation of the way things are. In fact, the focus of the jubilee on land, labour (slaves) and capital (debts) touches on what modern economics identifies as the three essential factors of production, which determine how power is distributed in society. The jubilee call for restitution, release and remission aims at a comprehensive act of reconciliation, of establishing right relationships with God in the community and with nature.

Earlier I referred to the growing recognition that human community and its relationship with nature can be sustained only if there are rules to limit power and greed. The idea that sustainability requires us to practise an ethic of self-limitation, a new form of "asceticism", lay behind ecumenical efforts, in the context of the Justice, Peace and Integrity of

Creation discussion, to formulate criteria to ensure the compatibility of our ways of living and acting with the need to maintain the ecological balance and the natural life-cycles, to respect the rights of the poor, the powerless and the refugees at home and internationally, and to safeguard the basis of life for future generations.

The biblical jubilee tradition provides the model of a community which periodically breaks the cycle of domination and exploitation in society and in its relationship with nature. The basic principle is that those in power who control the factors of production — land, labour and capital — are required to give up (forgive), to let go (release) and to allow those who are dependent to regain their rights and their dignity.

The jubilee principle thus not only contradicts the basic logic of the economy but also seems to undermine the political order by challenging the legitimacy of power based on acquired rights, especially property rights. The jubilee principle is an expression of the biblical logic of justice, which aims at right and sustainable relationships in community. The well-being of all takes precedence over the prosperity of the individual; and all members of the community, even animals and the land which are needed to sustain life, have their just claims to be respected in their dignity.

The jubilee principle thus provides the basic elements of an ethic of self-limitation, an ethic of enough, an ethic of being in relationships, of conversion, of regeneration. This ethic is rooted in the biblical understanding of God's justice, forgiveness and concern for the poor and for the well-being of the entire creation. Far from painting an idealized picture of a totally egalitarian society, the jubilee tradition can give us essential guidelines for building sustainable human communities. It can thus serve as orientation for the mission of the church in a world in which human communities are breaking up under the impact of a distorted value system which fosters production at the expense of reproduction, growth at the expense of conservation and regeneration, individual consumption at the expense of satisfying the needs of the majority, competition at the expense of maintaining relationships.

The call to conversion

These explorations of the biblical jubilee motif led naturally to the conclusion that the theme of the WCC's eighth assembly should be a clear invitation to an "ecumenical jubilee". To capture the spirit of the biblical jubilee in the context of the WCC's 50th anniversary, the central committee chose the theme "Turn to God — Rejoice in Hope". Its twofold emphasis — on conversion in the sense of *metanoia* and on expectant hope — seems to respond well to the condition of the ecumenical movement on the eve of a new millennium. In the remainder of this chapter, we shall concentrate on the first part of the theme and look more closely at its second part in the following chapter.

The appeal to "turn to God" reverberates throughout the witness of the biblical prophets. The prophetic call is to conversion, to a turning away from allegiance to false gods and to the God of the covenant. "Turn back to him whom you have deeply betrayed, O people of Israel" (Isa. 31:6). "Turn to me and be saved, all the ends of the earth! For I am God, and there is no other" (Isa. 45:22). Often it takes the form of an urgent invitation: "Return to me, for I have redeemed you" (Isa. 44:22); or, "Return to me, says the Lord of hosts, and I will return to you" (Zech. 1:3). This two-way covenant relationship between God and the people is echoed in the many Psalms which invoke God's faithfulness and urge God to turn graciously towards those in need (cf. Pss 25:16; 69:16; 80:14, 18; 86:16). Trust in God's faithfulness, even in times of defeat and despair, then leads to the resolve: "Come, let us return to the Lord; for it is he who has torn, and he will heal us; he has struck down, and he will bind us up. After two days he will revive us; on the third day he will raise us up, that we may live before him" (Hosea 6:1-2).

The assembly theme seeks to emphasize this comprehensive understanding of turning to God in the sense of entering anew into the covenant relationship, trusting in God's faithfulness, but also turning away from all that is contrary to God's will. In the New Testament one of the ways in which the Hebrew word for "turning to God" (*shub*) is rendered is by the Greek term *metanoia*. Central to the message of Jesus, it appears mainly in the synoptic gospels and Acts, but rarely in other parts of the New Testament. In John's gospel, Jesus refers to the same life-changing reality in terms of the process of "being born from above" (John 3:3).

Metanoia speaks of a radical change in one's understanding of the world and oneself, a reorientation not only of the mind, but of the entire being, a change of allegiance committing oneself to doing the will of God and adapting oneself to the values of God's realm (cf. Acts 5:31; 11:18; 26:20). "He has told you, O mortal, what is good; and what does the Lord require of you but to do justice and to love kindness, and to walk humbly with your God?" (Micah 6:8). For Jesus, the will of God was supremely expressed in the double commandment of love: "'You shall love the Lord your God with all your heart, and with all your soul, and with all your mind.' This is the greatest and first commandment. And the second is like it: You shall love your neighbour as yourself.' On these two commandments hang all the law and the prophets" (Matt. 22:37-40).

There is also a second term in the Greek New Testament (*epistrephein*) which renders more immediately the Hebrew meaning of turning around from a wrong way. It points to conversion as a continuous act rather than a one-time event. Thus the disciples and Peter are reminded by Jesus of the need to change, to turn around in order to remain on the way of discipleship (Matt. 18:3; Luke 22:32).

Ecumenical reflection on repentance, *metanoia* and conversion has been complicated by the particular understanding of it developed in the pietistic and revival tradition of Protestantism, which had a strong influence on the missionary movement. This concept moves from the recognition of one's sinfulness through active repentance to personal dedication to Christ — often expressed in terms of a "decision to accept Christ as one's personal saviour". Under the influence of the account in the Acts of the Apostles of the earliest Christian mission, conversion in this sense came to be understood as the heart of mission. This accent on personal salvation and the strongly moral connotation given to repentance — which is predominant in large parts of the evangelical Protestant tradition — is foreign to Orthodox spirituality.

The formulation of the eighth assembly theme, like the study document on "Conversion to God and Service to Man" prepared for the WCC's Uppsala assembly in 1968, seeks to situate this particular interpretation of repentance and conversion within a broader biblical context. Taking the biblical witness as a whole, one can identify the following elements as important for a contemporary understanding of conversion.

— Turning to God in conversion is not the first but the second act. Conversion is possible because God has first turned to this world in love and has become present in Jesus Christ for all of humanity.

— Conversion, the human response to God's turning, is an expression of trust in God's faithfulness. At the same time, it means turning away from the evil and destructive powers. Conversion aims at a transformation not only of the mind, but of the entire being.

— Conversion, while intensely personal, never remains an exclusively individual experience. It finds its expression by the incorporation of the person into a new community. Turning to God becomes visible in doing God's will. The biblical witness does not separate the individual from the social dimensions of conversion, repentance and sanctification.

— Conversion implies a new understanding of reality in the perspective of the kingdom of God. The personal aspect of being "born from above" and the affirmation of a new creation are corresponding features of the same reality. Each conversion, therefore, is a manifestation of God's eschatological act.

The conversion of churches

The call to conversion (*metanoia*) was a central theme of the conciliar process for Justice, Peace and the Integrity of Creation. The focal point of the documents from the ecumenical assembly in Dresden which culminated the JPIC process in the former German Democratic Republic was a penetrating interpretation of the call to conversion as a call to turn to and enter into God's shalom, which embraces justice, peace and the integrity of creation. God draws near to us in Jesus Christ, and the call to *metanoia* leads us not back into the past but forward into the future, into the promise of life. In the light of God's offer of *metanoia* we can recognize the true nature of the threats to life and confess our responsibility for the present crisis of the world. Thus our whole life, in both its individual and its social and historical dimensions, is addressed.

The final document of the European Ecumenical Assembly in Basel in 1989 followed the same line, including a central section on "Confession of Sin and Conversion to God". Responding to God's call to *metanoia* is more than merely accepting forgiveness. Our conversion to God demands that we turn actively towards God's justice, embrace God's shalom and live in harmony with God's entire creation. This understanding is then unfolded in a commitment and obligation to *move away* from divisions and separations, discrimination, violence and exploitation, and to *move towards* an inclusive society in which all find their place and the diversity of cultures and traditions is respected, a society marked by active nonviolence and a caring relationship to nature, a true community of women and men and a renewed church which lives out of continuing forgiveness.

The preamble to the final document of the 1990 world convocation on JPIC in Seoul includes a paragraph on repentance and conversion which emphasizes how radical is the reorientation required if a way is to be found out of the present predicament of the world:

> God confronts all of us with a call to repentance and conversion..., but this call does not mean the same for all. Jesus' call

to life took many forms — for the rich, it meant to get free from Mammon; for the sick, it meant to believe in God's love and healing power; for the privileged, it meant to share wealth and power; for the downtrodden, it meant to overcome despair; for the educated, it meant to renounce the pride of superiority; for the weak, it meant to gain self-confidence.

Today as well Jesus' call takes different forms. We live in radically different conditions, and are still far from having understood the implications of these differences. But at the same time, Jesus' call is addressed to us through today's threats. Repentance and conversion have become essential for survival... We are accountable to one another and need one another to learn who we are before God.

In an even more fundamental way, the call to conversion is the heart of the ecumenical movement. The affirmation of the first world conference on Life and Work in Stockholm in 1925 is well-known: "The closer we draw to the cross of Christ, the closer we come to each other." Important as doctrinal convergences and agreements are, the unity of the church will remain a distant goal without a genuine conversion — that is, a turning away from the negative images and exclusive identities fostered by the anathemas and mutual condemnations of the past — and a common turning to God in Christ as the only true foundation of our identity as Christians and churches. Unity as koinonia is first and foremost God's gift. We are called to receive this gift in the spirit of renewal and conversion of heart and mind.

In his encyclical *Ut unum sint*, Pope John Paul II recalls the affirmation of the Second Vatican Council that a change of heart and mind is the soul of the ecumenical movement: "There can be no ecumenism worthy of the name without a change of heart" (Decree on Ecumenism, para. 7). The entire encyclical is an invitation to place this call to personal and communal conversion at the very centre of the commitment to ecumenism. The pope sees ecumenical dialogue as intimately related to common prayer for one another and the examination of conscience in the spirit of repentance:

The Catholic Church must enter into what might be called a "dialogue of conversion", which constitutes the spiritual foundation of ecumenical dialogue... The "dialogue of conversion" with the Father on the part of each community, with the full acceptance of all that it demands, is the basis of fraternal relations which will be something more than a mere cordial understanding or external sociability... Only the act of placing ourselves before God can offer a solid basis for that conversion of individual Christians and for that constant reform of the church, insofar as she is also a human and earthly institution, which represent the precondition for all ecumenical commitment (para. 82).

The most sustained examination of the ecumenical significance of the call to conversion has come from the French ecumenical study group known as the Groupe des Dombes in its report *For the Conversion of the Churches* (1991; English translation, Geneva, WCC Publications, 1993). This document specifically addresses the churches' fear that the call to renewal and conversion threatens their identity and must be rejected out of loyalty to the truth as received and defined authoritatively. With a penetrating biblical and historical analysis it shows that identity and conversion are inseparable:

> There is no identity without conversion; *a fortiori*, Christian identity could not be constituted and sustained, either personally or ecclesially, without constant and continued conversion. That is the price of Christian identity. Conversion is at the heart of this.
>
> Essentially, *metanoia* is not aimed here at failings or marginal faults — of which the churches must also repent. It concerns their confessions of faith, precisely where the churches call themselves in the fullest sense of the term "Catholic" or "Orthodox" or "Protestant", but also where these designations concern apparently non-negotiable elements of their faith (p.4).

The report interprets the whole ecumenical movement as a process of "conversion underway", focusing particularly on the conversion and transformation of confessional identities. It sees the four credal "marks of the church" — unity, holiness, catholicity and apostolicity — as an invitation to critical self-examination and conversion. It also identifies some decisive steps the churches should take in this process of conversion, including agreement on a common version of the traditional creeds, a lifting of those historical anathemas which no longer affect the partners of today, reception of the doctrinal agreements already reached during the last 25 years and application of these in their life, beginning with public and liturgical acts of forgiveness and reconciliation.

Elements of an ecumenical jubilee

If the eighth assembly of the WCC and its theme are interpreted as an invitation to an ecumenical jubilee, what might this mean for the churches? Building on the biblical explorations and ecumenical reflections about conversion developed in this chapter, we may identify a number of aspects of this.

1. An ecumenical jubilee would mean seizing the anniversary year of the World Council of Churches as a year of "God's favour", a time under God's promise. This sense of a *kairos* which is rooted in an affirmation of God's faithfulness is included in the invitation "Turn to God" — an echo of the biblical call to *metanoia* as repentance and conversion which interrupt the flow of "business as usual" and affirm God as the source of life, wholeness and hope. Turning to God suggests a change of allegiance, a liberation from other powers and captivities. It echoes the continuing reinterpretation and reappropriation of the biblical sabbath and jubilee year traditions as expressions of hope for fulfilment of the expectation of life in its fullness, of which the jubilee year is a symbol: "Today in your hearing this message is fulfilled... Now is the time!"

2. The jubilee signifies a return to the covenant order of God. It is noteworthy that all the key concepts linked with the jubilee begin with the prefix "re-": remission, release, restitution, restoration, reconstruction, repentance, reconciliation. Yet rather than a turning backwards, this "re-turn" (*metanoia*) is a reordering of life and a reorientation which shows the way out of the "house of slavery" (Ex. 20:2) into

the household of life. It is an invitation to "return to the future", to be liberated from the bonds of the past and to embrace the promise of life. The appeal of the Groupe des Dombes for a "conversion of the churches" is based on the conviction that the churches' particular identities, marked as they are by the history of division, need to be transformed by a process of turning to the common source of their identity, which is Jesus Christ. Conversion, therefore, means being liberated from the bonds which tie the churches to their past and turning to Christ who is always ahead of us.

3. The ecumenical jubilee is a call for the reordering of the churches' life, for mutual forgiveness and reconciliation and for the restoration of communion. The jubilee ordinance for the restitution of ancestral land is rooted in the affirmation that the land belongs to God and the members of God's people are only trustees of it and tenants on it (Lev. 25:23). For the early Christians, who began as a fringe group on the margins of the recognized Jewish community, especially in the diaspora, the decisive affirmation was they were no longer aliens or strangers, but full members of God's household (Eph. 2:19; 1 Peter 2:4-10). The household belongs to God, and there is no privileged access or exclusive titles. An ecumenical jubilee would mean rendering the life of the church, of the ecumenical movement, back into the hands of God, cancelling all debts, all mutual condemnations, and being released into the glorious liberty of the children of God.

The continuing separation of the churches is deeply rooted in unconfessed and unforgiven sin and guilt. What separates the churches is not only doctrine and practice, but also their acquiescence in division and their defence of particular identities. Forgiveness therefore requires a reconciliation of memories through an active and common remembrance of the past. This could be extended to a liberation from the feelings of guilt growing out of 500 years of European colonization and 200 years of Western missionary expansion. Such a confession of guilt and acceptance of forgiveness and reconciliation are particularly relevant at the end of the 20th century, which has been both the most destructive period in human history and the time when the church rediscovered its ecumenical calling. The eighth assembly could thus provide the framework for a litany of confession, forgiveness and reconciliation — an act of unity at the end of the millennium of division and Christian expansion, leading up to a reaffirmation of the ecumenical covenant of the churches.

4. Only churches which have themselves responded to the jubilee call and reordered their lives and relationships accordingly can dare to direct the jubilee call to the wider human community. A test case of this is the Ecumenical Decade — Churches in Solidarity with Women, which comes to its conclusion during the same year as the assembly. In many churches, this Decade has been a period of painful self-examination. It has brought to the surface the widespread reality of not only discrimination but also violence against women in church and society. Will the culmination of the Decade provide evidence that the churches are ready to respond to the call for the restoration of community in the one household of God?

Central to the biblical jubilee is the self-limitation of power as exercised in control over land, labour and capital in order to restore a sustainable order of human community. Violence in all its forms is an expression of the uncontrolled excess of power which destroys relationships in human community. The churches are called to live as jubilee communities. Reappropriation of the biblical jubilee tradition would thus serve as a strong reinforcement of the ecumenical commitment to work towards overcoming violence.

5. Ecumenical reflection about a theology of life, the focus of continued discussion of the issues raised by the JPIC process, could be sharpened by the jubilee emphasis on the redistribution of land. The earth, the land, belongs to God, who provides for our livelihood; and all people are entitled to what they need. This biblical affirmation leads to the impera-

tive to redistribute the land, to cease productive activity and to give the land back to God from whom it was received. In this way, the integrity of creation is restored and the sanctity of life as a gift from God is respected. An ecumenical jubilee would mean accepting a new form of life which reflects a deepened understanding of God's creation and of humanity's place within it. The WCC's seventh assembly (Canberra 1991) called for a new ethic of economy and ecology, in which the orientation towards growth and consumption is replaced by the values of sustainability and use. Heightened recognition of the disastrous consequences of accelerated climate change has made us even more aware of the need for a profound social, political and spiritual reorientation, a genuine conversion to a new system of values. An ecumenical jubilee could become the occasion for the churches to commit themselves to this change.

6. Leviticus 25 places the announcement of the jubilee in the framework of liturgy and worship. Its opening moment is the sound of the trumpet on the day of atonement. In this sense the whole jubilee legislation can be interpreted as guidelines for what has come to be called the "liturgy after the liturgy". This is echoed in what the prophets say about true worship, expressed perhaps most eloquently in Isaiah 58, which Jesus later affirmed in his teaching about the sabbath (Mark 2:23-28). Subsequently the patristic tradition interpreted the jubilee, in the light of the resurrection and the outpouring of the Spirit, as the manifestation of the time of salvation, of the fullness of life offered by God. This could serve to deepen ecumenical reflection on the inseparability of worship and spirituality on the one hand and the effort to rebuild human community on the other. If the assembly were to lead to a solemn recommitment by the churches to a life which corresponds to the message of Jesus in his first sermon in Nazareth, the ecumenical jubilee of the year 1998 could be continued in preparing the churches for the year 2000 in the spirit of true worship, binding together spirituality and the commitment to restoring right relationships in human community.

Towards the Year 2000

The symbolic date of the year 2000 and its significance for understanding the mission of the church at this moment in history have been underscored by Pope John Paul II in his apostolic letter *Tertio Millennio Adveniente*. The letter places the celebration of the "Great Jubilee" of the 2000th anniversary of the birth of Jesus Christ in the wider context of the history of salvation and of the church's continuation of the biblical practice of commemorating God's great deeds among God's people. In the Catholic tradition, this has happened especially during the so-called "Holy Years", celebrated every fifty years since around 1300.

The pope's explication of the biblical jubilee in this letter unfolds the rich meaning of this motif and then translates it into the outline for a process of spiritual and liturgical preparation to raise awareness among Christians of the "value and meaning of the jubilee of the year 2000 in human history" (para. 31). This begins with an examination of conscience regarding how the church and its members have failed in their mission during these last ten centuries: the divisions among the Christian churches, their intolerance and even violence in defending the truth, their complicity in countless acts of injustice and exclusion. All of this has become a counter-witness and a scandal; thus, any joyful celebration of a jubilee must begin with a genuine movement of conversion.

The second phase of preparation for the jubilee follows the trinitarian confession, with three successive years (1997-1999) consecrated to the contemplation of Jesus Christ, the Holy Spirit and God the Father, and focusing on the theological virtues of faith, hope and love. An ecumenical intention permeates the whole presentation, inviting Christians to turn together to Christ, the one Lord, and to strengthen their common witness; to celebrate the Spirit as the source of hope and unity; and to work together for a "*civilization of love*, founded on the universal values of peace, solidarity, justice and liberty, which find their full attainment in Christ" (para. 52).

This apostolic letter forcefully expresses the hope that the year 2000 might be an occasion for a strong affirmation of Christian unity. The churches cannot in good conscience commemorate the birth of Jesus Christ 2000 years ago unless they acknowledge together this ecumenical calling and make courageous efforts to overcome the barriers which still separate them from one another. In this spirit, the pope suggests a meeting of all Christians to reflect the ecumenical and universal character of this jubilee. "This would be an event of great significance, and so, in order to avoid misunderstandings, it should be properly presented and carefully prepared, in an attitude of fraternal cooperation with Christians of other denominations and traditions, as well as of grateful openness to those religions whose representatives might wish to acknowledge the joy shared by all the disciples of Christ" (para. 55). Furthermore, the pope suggests that ways might be found to arrange historic meetings "in places of exceptional symbolic importance like Bethlehem, Jerusalem and Mount Sinai as a means of furthering dialogue with Jews and the followers of Islam... and similar meetings elsewhere with the leaders of the great world religions" (para. 53).

The initiative taken by the pope in this letter has certainly helped to focus attention on the significance of the year 2000 among Christian people far beyond the Roman Catholic Church. Various plans and proposals are now under discussion, particularly among the Eastern Orthodox churches, in the Church of England and in the Anglican Communion, among the secretaries of Christian World Communions, and also among evangelical groups and organizations. Many of these plans focus on the year 2000 as an occasion for renewed evangelization at a time of a growing marginalization of the Christian churches in the life of their societies.

In keeping with its mandate to strengthen relationships between the churches, the World Council of Churches has taken the initiative to bring together representatives of all churches and groups known to be engaged in preparations for the year 2000, to share information and explore the possibilities of ecumenical cooperation. The response to this initiative has been positive, and there is hope that the possibilities offered by the year 2000 for a genuinely common witness and for a renewed commitment to the unity of the church can be realized.

Such a commemoration will be a witness to Jesus Christ as the source of faith, hope and love only if it addresses the hopes and fears, expectations and anxieties among people today in view of the changes affecting their lives as the third millennium approaches. Important as it is to remember the way of the church during the outgoing millennium in a spirit of repentance and joyful celebration, what is essential will be engaging together in discerning the signs of the time, so that the commemoration of the year 2000 might become an invitation to a renewal in the life and witness of the church.

5. Joy and Hope

Anniversaries in the life of any individual or community are times for rejoicing and celebration. Temporarily liberated from everyday chores and in the company of friends, we can renew the bonds of community and experience something of the fullness of life. All cultures have their own rituals to mark significant anniversaries. These include acts of common recollection of the past, retelling, chanting or acting out its stories. In most cultures sharing a festive meal is an indispensable part of celebrating an anniversary, as is a liturgy of thanksgiving to God for sustaining and protecting the individual or community until this moment.

Celebrating an anniversary is an activity that takes place in a time and space which are set apart. Food and drink are saved for the occasion. In celebration, human beings are able to transcend the scarcities and limitations of everyday life. Joy is the emotion which expresses the experience of overflowing abundance and gratuity of life.

Anniversaries and seasonal festivals mark the rhythmic flow of time. They break the dominance of the linear, goal-directed progression of time, and provide moments for re-creation and re-generation. In the Christian tradition the liturgical year from Advent to Pentecost re-enacts in remembrance and celebration the significant events in the human life of Christ. In the Jewish tradition the sabbath is not only the day of rest, mirroring God's own rest on the seventh day of creation, but also an occasion for joyful celebration. The Christian church began to mark Sunday, the first day of the week, as the regular remembrance of the resurrection, the beginning of life in the new creation. The joy associated with the celebration of the eucharist was recognized as a foretaste of the feast to come in God's kingdom and of the promised fullness of life.

Jesus lived his ministry of preaching and healing in the joy of the kingdom. In his presence, there was no place for fasting; rather, he invited people to the joy of the wedding feast (Mark 2:18-20; cf. John 2:1-11). The open invitation to the festive meal became a parable of the kingdom of God which had drawn near (Matt. 22:2-10). That meant Jesus did not hesitate to share table fellowship with those whom the religious authorities dismissed as sinners (Matt. 9:11; Luke 15:2). Indeed, it was a cause of joy when those considered lost and outside the covenant community turned to him in trust and expectation, for "there will be more joy in heaven over one sinner who repents [literally, turns around] than over ninety-nine righteous persons who need no repentance" (Luke 15:7). Later in the same chapter this joy which accompanies the event of true *metanoia* resonates from the parable of the prodigal son, culminating in the concluding words of the father: "We *had to celebrate and rejoice* because this brother of yours was dead and has come to life; he was lost and has been found" (v. 32).

Something to celebrate

Should the 50th anniversary of the WCC be an occasion for joy and celebration? When the central committee discussed the formulation of the theme of the assembly, opinions were divided on this point. Some members suggested that the precarious situation of their own churches and people would inhibit them from joining a celebration. Some argued that in the present situation of ecumenical uncertainty and stagnation a sober atmosphere of critical self-assessment would be more appropriate than an act of festive and confident self-affirmation. Perhaps one can also detect in this reaction a certain influence of Protestant puritanism, which has always made the WCC notoriously suspicious of any sign of "triumphalism". It could be salutary from time to time to look at the many communities of poor people who engage in joyful celebrations as an affirmation of life precisely in the midst of deprivation.

In the end, however, it is not our personal assessment of the contemporary situation of the WCC but the inner dynamic of the assembly theme itself which leads ineluctably from the movement of conversion to joyful celebration and thanksgiving. Just as our turning to God is a response to

God's having turned in Christ towards the world, so celebrating the 50th anniversary of the WCC does not mean congratulating ourselves. It is rather an act of celebration and thanksgiving for God's work among the churches through the Spirit, who has liberated the churches from their self-isolation and enabled them to rediscover their unity in Christ. It is in celebration and thanksgiving that we affirm God as the source of vitality in the ecumenical movement, that we open ourselves to and prepare ourselves for the continuing process of conversion. In joyful celebration, we put aside for a moment our plans and programmes and strategies, our efforts to produce ever new conceptions of unity and models of union, and allow ourselves to be transformed by God's Spirit. In our celebration we finally anticipate that moment when we shall be able "with one voice [to] glorify God, the Father of our Lord Jesus Christ" (Rom 15:6).

The call to conversion must not end with the examination of our conscience and the admission of our failures — important and indispensable as these are. In fact, the true confession of our failings does not precede but grows out of our confession of trust in the faithfulness of God. Our trust in God's forgiveness and gratuitous love liberates us to look at our own brokenness without defensiveness. Apart from the invitation to joyful celebration, the call to conversion remains exposed to the temptation of self-righteousness, even to the extent of dismissing the real changes which the ecumenical movement has brought about in the churches' relationships to one another. One could even say that the churches' inability or unwillingness to acknowledge these signs of renewal with gratitude and joy is a major impediment to their moving forward.

We have inherited the ecumenical movement from the generations which have gone before us. Their witness needs to be recalled and retold. The hopes and visions are being reshaped from one generation to the next. There is no viable hope apart from memory; and the reconciliation of memories releases energies for new hope.

Biblical perspectives on hope

The appeal to "rejoice in hope" is taken from Paul's letter to the Romans (Rom. 12:15). Opening the final part of his letter, Paul refers to the process of conversion as the source of a new life in community. "Do not be conformed to this world, but be transformed by the renewing of your minds, so that you may discern what is the will of God — what is good and acceptable and perfect" (Rom. 12:2). A long series of exhortations follows, all of them pointing to the qualities of relationship by which the community manifests its calling to be "one body in Christ" (v.5).

Earlier in the same letter, Paul has cited Abraham as an example of hope. Abraham trusted in the God "who gives life to the dead and calls into existence the things that do not exist. Hoping against hope, he believed that he would become 'the father of many nations'... No distrust made him waver concerning the promise of God" (Rom. 4:17f.,20). Similarly, he speaks of the entire creation as living in the attitude of hope for the fulfilment of God's promise (Rom. 8:19ff.). It is God's Spirit who keeps hope alive. "For in hope we were saved. Now hope that is seen is not hope. For who hopes for what is seen? But if we hope for what we do not see, we wait for it with patience" (Rom. 8:24f.).

The most vivid expression of the movement from conversion to new hope is found in the doxology which opens the first letter of Peter. It is worth quoting at length:

> Blessed be the God and Father of our Lord Jesus Christ! By his great mercy he has given us a new birth into a living hope through the resurrection of Jesus Christ from the dead, and into an inheritance that is imperishable... In this you rejoice, even if now for a little while you have had to suffer various trials, so that the genuineness of your faith... may be found to result in praise and glory and honour when Jesus Christ is revealed. Although you have not seen him, you love him; and even though you do not see him now, you believe in him and rejoice with indescribable and glorious joy, for you are receiving the outcome of your faith, the salvation of your souls (1 Peter 1:3-9).

The expressive language of this doxology could make us forget the precarious conditions under which the original recipients of this letter, which was a kind of ecumenical encyclical to Christian communities in Asia Minor, were living. The position of Asia Minor in the Roman empire during the first and second centuries was in many ways similar to the geopolitical situation of many countries in the southern hemisphere today. Paul had begun his missionary work here, mainly among the Jewish diaspora; and from his letters and the Acts of the Apostles we know something of these early Christian communities, their internal struggles and their search for a firm identity.

By the time of the first letter of Peter, usually dated about one generation after Paul, they were still small minority communities scattered in the diaspora (1 Pet. 1:1), like "aliens and exiles" in a foreign land (2:11). Apparently, however, they were strong enough to have become the target of persecution. The main concern of this letter is to strengthen and encourage them in the great suffering they are going through (1 Pet. 4:12), by holding before them the example of Christ their Lord, "for Christ also suffered for sins once for all, the righteous for the unrighteous, in order to bring you to God. He was put to death in the flesh, but made alive in the spirit" (1 Pet. 3:18). And those who suffer because they walk in the way of Christ also share in his glory.

Thus, while suffering pervaded the lives of these communities, the basic tone of this letter to them is one of hope — not in the sense of an attitude of expectancy of something which might happen in the future, but as an inner assurance growing out of trust in God's faithfulness. The hope of which this letter speaks will survive the test of fire (1 Pet. 1:7) and generates resistance against even the most threatening forces (5:8ff.).

What is the foundation, the origin of this hope? The doxology cited above provides the answer: God "has given us a new birth into a living hope through the resurrection of Jesus Christ from the dead" (1 Pet. 1:3). This is the centre of our Christian faith, and it distinguishes the living hope from "merely human hopes". For, as Paul wrote to the Christians in Corinth, "If with merely human hopes I fought with wild animals at Ephesus, what would I have gained by it?" (1 Cor. 15:32). The resurrection of Christ from the dead is the beginning of new life for all who put their trust in him. Therefore, "if *for this life only* we have hoped in Christ, we are of all people most to be pitied" (1 Cor. 15:19). All merely human hopes are under the threat of being disappointed and revealed as dead hopes. The living hope through the resurrection of Christ from the dead is the manifestation of a new life, the consequence of being born anew, of having turned around to God.

The "living hope" of which Paul and Peter speak is therefore not a pious promise; it is an "inheritance" (1 Pet. 1:4), which no one can take away from those who have received the new life from God. But just as this living hope stands in contrast to and in tension with all "merely human hopes", so the new life which is sustained by its breath remains a life of struggle and potential suffering. While the new reality of life in its fullness has been revealed in the resurrection of Christ from the dead and has become part of our human life, we live this new life "in hope". We are still exposed to the powers of death, but we have the certain assurance that death will not speak the final word, that there is an alternative to the dominant system and its dynamics of exclusion. The most powerful symbol of this "living hope" is the reign of God, which Jesus proclaimed in his parables and made a living reality in his life and ministry of healing. It is in and through this "living hope" that the many martyrs of our time have been sustained in their struggles, even to the point of giving their own lives. They have thus become for us the sustainers of our hope; they have become like the grain of wheat that needs to die in order to bear fruit (John 12:24).

This brief meditation on the biblical understanding of hope would be incomplete without a reference to the letter to the Ephesians, written to communities in the same region and living under very similar conditions as those to whom the first letter of Peter was sent. Among their neighbours these people "were the first to set [their] hope on Christ" (Eph. 1:12). But this faith had to be nurtured and strengthened, "so that, with the eyes of your heart enlightened, you may know what is the hope to which he has called you, what are the riches of his glorious inheritance among the saints" (Eph. 1:18). The letter refers to its addressees as "sharers in the promise" (Eph. 3:6). This promise, the hope to which they have been called, is not something static, but a dynamic reality in history. There is, first, the movement from then to now, and from "at one time" to the present. "Remember that you were at that time without Christ, being aliens from the commonwealth of Israel, and strangers to the covenants of promise, having no hope and without God in the world" (Eph. 2:12). Now, in Christ, a total change has taken place — but not by any effort or merit on their own part: "For by grace you have been saved through faith...; it is the gift of God... For we are what he has made us, created in Christ Jesus for good works" (Eph. 2:8-10). This new reality then continues to grow like a building that is rising from its own foundations (cf. Eph. 2:21f.).

The hope which now animates their lives is rooted in the promise of God which they have inherited and in which they share. This promise has been the focus of God's covenant with God's people from the time of Noah through Abraham and David until the new covenant in the blood of Christ. From the beginning, the divine purpose has been to bind together God, humanity and all of creation in a living communion, so that — in the fullness of time — God might "gather up all things in him, things in heaven and things on earth" (Eph. 1:10). The creation of one body, establishing a commonwealth of free citizens out of the separated and disjointed members, is a present revelation of God's promise. Those who share in this promise become themselves bearers, signs, living manifestations of the new reality. This promise is not something one can share in alone, privately, spiritually. The images of the body, the commonwealth, the household, the temple building all point to the new community at the very core of the promise, which is a relational, social reality.

Throughout the letter to the Ephesians, it is clear that the unity of this new humanity — of the one body and the one household — is the work of God's Spirit within us, who is able "to accomplish abundantly far more than all we can ask or imagine" (Eph. 3:20). For us, it remains a gift and a calling, to which we are to respond by leading a life "worthy of the calling to which you have been called" (Eph. 4:1). And we are strengthened in our efforts to "maintain the unity of the Spirit and the bond of peace" in and through "the one hope of [our] calling" (Eph. 4:3-4).

It would limit the scope of this vision to apply it only to relationships within and between the communities of those who follow Christ and who have been united with him through baptism in faith. The purpose of God, the ultimate aim of God's promise, is to "create in Christ one new humanity in the place of two" (Eph. 2:15). All those who are still aliens and strangers to the covenants of promise are ultimately to be included. In the purpose of God, the unity of the church is inseparable from the unity of humankind: fellowship in the household of God is to be a sign for the *shalom* — the sense of peace, justice and the well-being of creation — which God wants to establish through Christ among all created beings.

Because God's promise is to gather up all things in heaven and on earth, to restore the wholeness of God's creation, the hope which shares in this promise cannot but reflect the nature of what is being hoped for. The common calling, which is addressed to all those who believe in Christ, establishes a new community of hope which becomes a source of hope to the wider community around it.

It is this common calling which the eighth assembly theme reaffirms in inviting us to "rejoice in hope".

Ecumenical reflections on hope

From the outset the ecumenical movement may be seen as an effort by the churches to respond to this call for conversion into a living hope. They have not, however, found it easy to give a common account of the hope that inspires them in their fellowship with one another. In preparing for the eighth assembly, it may be helpful to recall some issues and insights from three earlier ecumenical discussions of Christian hope.

The first is that of the WCC's second assembly (Evanston 1954), whose theme was "Christ, the Hope of the World" and whose message to the churches in fact closed with the words "Therefore, we call on you: rejoice in hope!" While the key motif of the work of the Evanston assembly was the affirmation that "our hope is Jesus Christ", the intensive preparatory theological discussions in the consultative committee on the assembly theme — which had brought together some of the leading theologians of the day — disclosed profound differences in understanding the Christian hope. For some, this hope was essentially eschatological, otherworldly. Others wanted to interpret Christian hope as a powerful dynamic shaping history and society.

The report on the main theme compared the Christian hope with secular expressions of hope in democratic and scientific-technological humanism, in Marxism, in the national and religious renaissance in Asia and Africa, as well as with the brave nihilism of those without any hope. The report treated these rival hopes sensitively and modestly — while conveying an unperturbed confidence in the universal truth of the Christian message of hope. In its response to the report the assembly in fact felt that it had not sounded clearly enough the note of joyful certainty and radiant expectation which should characterize a statement about Christian hope.

Yet in the work of its sections, the Evanston assembly was fully aware of the challenges of the time: the threat of the cold war and the manifestation of ethnic and racial tensions in many parts of the world. Its discussions of Christian hope did not divert its attention from the "fear and distrust which at present divide the world". The search for the unity of the church was also set in the perspective of Christian hope: "At Amsterdam we said that we intend to stay together. He has kept us together. He has shown himself again as our hope. Emboldened by this hope, we dedicate ourselves to God anew, that he may enable us to grow together."

The WCC in 1954 was still dominated by the perspective of the northern churches. The favoured model for the development of peoples and societies was obviously the Western ideal of a socially responsible, liberal democratic welfare system. But the Evanston assembly also recognized clearly the dangerous consequences of a confrontational stance over against communism, in particular the tendency in democratic societies to limit civil rights, to treat unpopular and critical opinions as subversive and to make military security an overarching priority.

Today we are discovering that the liberation of societies from what C.L. Patijn called the "dangerous illusions of utopianism and the bondage of political dogma" is not in itself the fulfilment of human hopes. In fact, the contemporary discrediting of all critical alternatives has created a situation in which we have become captives of a system which is almost obliged to reproduce itself and in which people, in particular the younger generation, seem to have difficulty even entertaining visions or dreaming dreams about a more just society. For many, the energy for hoping seems to have been exhausted by the effort to preserve and defend the acquired way of living. Even the hopes of democratic and scientific humanism which were discussed in the consultative committee on the main theme of the Evanston Assembly appear to have lost their power of inspiration.

Some twenty years after the Evanston assembly, the WCC's commission on Faith and Order began a process of reflecting about and accounting for the hope that is in us. Rather than starting from a biblical-theological exposition of Christian hope, this study asked groups of Christians from various contexts, including women and youth, to articulate their hopes as Christian people today. One thing this exercise showed is how intensely personal and contextual the language of hope is. It is not easy to harmonize our different accounts of hope; and in many instances our hopes challenge one another. What is a source of hope for some is a cause of fear and disquiet to others.

When these various accounts of hope were brought together, it became necessary to distinguish between hopes and desires or wishes, between the level at which specific things are hoped for — to have enough to eat, to have a home, to have a job — and the level at which the question arises as to why people hope at all in the face of all evidence.

Beyond this reality of mutual criticism and judgment, the final report of this study, adopted by the meeting of the Faith and Order commission in Bangalore in 1978, also sees the reality of mutual encouragement. In fact, we have experienced in many situations that we can become helpers of each other's hopes, that there is something like vicarious hope for those who have lost all hope, that hope is not a private, but a community affair. Particularly noteworthy is the constant transfer of energies of hope from the South to the North, from the poor to the rich, from those without power to those burdened by the responsibility of exercising power, from those who hope against all hope to those who do not know what to hope for because they have everything. This experience led the Bangalore meeting to the crucial affirmation in its account of hope: "The Christian hope is a resistance movement against fatalism."

The preamble to the "act of covenanting" in the final document from the WCC's world convocation on Justice, Peace and the Integrity of Creation (Seoul 1990) includes a paragraph entitled "A Community of Hope and Sharing", which echoes this affirmation from Bangalore. It can serve well to conclude this brief survey of ecumenical reflection on hope:

Conversion is the door to a new and firm hope — the conviction that the course of history can be changed. We are easily overcome by doubts: Has not power always had the last word? Are victims not inevitable? Are not war and hatred part of the human condition and therefore impossible to overcome? Is it not true that technological development has its own dynamics and therefore cannot be reversed and mastered? Christian hope is a resistance movement against fatalism. We want to share this hope with all people and join with them in the same movement. We want to learn from their experience and from the hope by which they are sustained in their struggle.

The uses of utopia

Less than ten years after Seoul, twenty years after Bangalore and more than forty years after Evanston, the appeal to "rejoice in hope" which concluded the message from Evanston comes to the eighth assembly under radically changed circumstances. There are no more rival hopes competing with each other. Even within the Christian churches, postmodern scepticism about all claims to a coherent and universally valid framework of meaning have made deep inroads. The experience of struggle, out of which the affirmation of Christian hope as a resistance movement against fatalism was formulated, seems to belong to another era. The dominant mood at the end of this century is shaped by the conviction, actively encouraged by the powerful, that there is no alternative to the system of the global market. Those excluded from the system are condemned to hopelessness. They are expendable.

This is the background against which the assembly in Harare will be invited to articulate afresh an ecumenical vision looking forward to the 21st century. We have seen that the biblical jubilee tradition, which Jesus appropriated in his first sermon at Nazareth, is to serve as a source of inspiration for the assembly, as the matrix for a new affirmation of the ecumenical vision. But can we today nourish — against all historical evidence — the hope that the jubilee principles might be put into practice? Indeed, most people would dismiss the prescriptions in Leviticus 25 as a classic case of utopian thinking. No society and no economy, they would tell us, could function and survive on the basis of these rules.

What distinguishes an ecumenical vision rooted in the expectant hope for God's kingdom and nourished by the good news proclaimed by Jesus in Nazareth from utopian thinking? The term "utopian" has come to be used almost exclusively to disparage the visionary character of any models or proposals for changing "the way things are". To be utopian is to be an idealist, a dreamer, to indulge in fantasies, to lose contact with reality. In a world governed by scientific calculation and the technological approach to "problem-solving", there seems to be no room for utopian thinking.

Many would pass the same verdict on the effort to formulate a vision for the ecumenical movement on the eve of the third millennium. The biblical idiom of hope has become a foreign language for the majority of the young generation, whose hopes and fears are rather directed to the immediate needs of life and survival. They have lost confidence in grand designs of the future, whether political, ideological or religious. And yet there is a longing to reach beyond the situation of fragmented and individualized hopes and perspectives on life. The end of the century and the dawning of a new millennium are creating a climate of anxious expectation. There seems to be no shortage of willing followers for religious movements which offer a seemingly coherent interpretation of the present against the background of a scenario of the end of time and history. Can the ecumenical vision be brought to life again so that it will inspire even a thoroughly disillusioned young generation?

The ecumenical movement of our century has had a strong utopian element. To speak of the unity of the church for the sake of the renewal of human community is indeed a utopian project: challenging the status quo of divided churches so that they might be transformed into signs of the new humanity in Christ. Ernst Lange's book *And Yet It Moves...* (1979, German original 1972) was a powerful apologia for "the utopian dream of a united and renewed Christendom which would be the 'leaven', the pattern, the stimulus of the coming world community, the custodian of a source of humanization, which is not only inexhaustible, but also always far in advance of every form of human achievement yet realized in history, namely, the humanity of Jesus of Nazareth" (p.9). Just as others have declared that the utopia of world peace is the prerequisite if our world, shaped by science and technology, is to have a future, so Ernst Lange proclaimed the ecumenical utopia as the critical test of what it means to be the church today.

But whether or not we appropriate the term "utopia" for the ecumenical vision, awareness of the context of utopian thinking can help us to see how a statement of the ecumenical vision might be received. The word itself comes from the name Thomas More gave to the imaginary island he created as the setting for the perfect society, depicted in his treatise of that name written in 1516. Since then it has been applied to an entire genre of literature. Writers and thinkers have constructed utopias particularly in periods of uncertainty and despair, often in the hope that the gap between the ideal they projected and the dismal reality of the status quo might generate the energy for change and transformation.

In our own century, writers such as Aldous Huxley (*Brave New World*) and George Orwell (*1984*) put this literary form to a very different use. The terrifying future societies they imagined were meant to expose the unacknow-ledged consequences of developments already taking place, and thus to unmask the fundamentally utopian character of the spirit of modernity. For instance, the idea that the global market economy creates "the best of all worlds" is itself a utopian claim — as is evident if we look at it from the perspective from below, the perspective of those who are excluded from enjoying its benefits. Unlike those utopias which challenge and subvert the status quo, the market utopia is an ideology that serves the interests of defending and expanding the power and domination of those who have it.

Having thus become captivated by a utopia turned into an ideology, which has blinded us to reality and its contradic-tions, should we not try to regain the critical sense of utopia? We must begin by questioning the commonsense assumption which contrasts utopian thinking with a "realistic" view of the world, for any perception of reality, especially social reality, is shaped and conditioned by the social position and the interests of those who speak or act. Utopian projections may thus serve as a critical test for reality as it is by unmasking the ideological element in what is considered "realistic" and by opening our eyes to the dangerous and destructive consequences which will ensue if the present course of events continues unchanged. In this sense the biblical prophets and their later followers engaged in utopian thinking.

This leads finally to the examples of utopian reflection which anticipate and describe a different future precisely to mobilize the potential for change and to liberate human community from captivity to the past and from a fatalistic sense of resignation that things will and in fact can never change. This kind of utopian thinking has an affinity to the mystical or prophetic dimension of religion expressed in the biblical visions of a new heaven and a new earth in Isaiah 65 and the book of Revelation. It is out of this context that Jesus' reappropriation of the jubilee tradition in his sermon in Nazareth as recorded in Luke 4 should be read.

In a novel published in 1942 entitled "We Are Utopia" (*Wir sind Utopia*), the German writer Stefan Andres takes us to Spain at the time of the civil war to tell the story of a former monk who is being held as a prisoner of war in the Carmelite monastery he had left twenty years earlier when the world of monastic life had become too narrow for him. Back in his previous cell, he remembers how he used to project an ideal island of bliss onto the ceiling of this very room. His spiritual father, an old mystic, had tried to convince him that none of these utopias had ever come true. Yet he had needed this projection in order to maintain the zeal of his faith, and so he had clung to it.

Before he had left the monastery, his spiritual father had given him a piece of advice: "God does not go to utopia! But he comes into this world, wet with tears — again and again! Because here there is infinite poverty, infinite hunger, infinite suffering! God loves the wholly Other, God loves the abyss... God loves this world because it is imperfect — we are God's utopia, but in the process of becoming!" Following this lead, the novel then gives a moving portrait of how

God's utopia became visible amidst war, betrayal and brutality in an act of forgiveness of sins and absolution given against all canonical rules and human insight.

The jubilee principle indeed contradicts established rules and human insights. But it opens the horizon for God's utopia which we are meant to become. If understood as a parable for God's utopia, for the new community in the kingdom of God, then the jubilee tradition can indeed become the matrix of an ecumenical vision.

Communities of hope

While the Evanston assembly in 1954 felt called to affirm Jesus Christ as the one hope of the world over against all the rival hopes of the time, the Faith and Order commission at Bangalore in 1978 struggled with the task of formulating a common account of hope in view of the diversity and even contradictions among accounts of Christian hope coming from many different contexts. The commission tried not only to articulate the content of Christian hope, but also to penetrate to its source, which nurtures the very act of hoping against all hope, which maintains the trust that reaches beyond the seemingly inescapable realities of the world.

The doxology at the beginning of the first letter of Peter, which we have cited earlier, refers to this source as the "new birth into a living hope through the resurrection of Jesus Christ from the dead". God's promise to create a new humanity has been manifested through the resurrection of Jesus Christ from the dead. As we are drawn into the power of the one who raised Jesus Christ from the dead, we are born again to a living hope. This hope is the breath of new life to which we are called. It is distinguished from those "merely human hopes" focused on specific things which we await anxiously or which we want to possess. It is hope precisely because it transcends what we can see, touch and possess. Christian hope stretches out towards that which is promised but not yet revealed. At the level of "merely human hopes", the hopes of one can become the source of anxiety or despair for the other, because we are different as human beings and live under different conditions. And since all relationships within the human community are shaped by the realities of power and powerlessness, our human hopes often divide instead of uniting us.

The appeal to "rejoice in hope" calls us to trust in the promise and faithfulness of God who has broken down the dividing wall and will unite all things so that God will be in all and through all. In the perspective of the letter to the Ephesians, hope is the trust and confidence that this coherence and wholeness of all that is will be fully revealed in God's own time. To this hope we are called as those who share in the Spirit of Christ who was raised from the dead. We can live and maintain this hope only if we keep "the unity of the Spirit in the bond of peace" (Eph. 4:3).

Our response to God's calling must therefore lead to the formation of communities of hope, to the reshaping of viable human communities even in the midst of the forces of disintegration and exclusion. In these communities, there will no longer be strangers and aliens, for all become members of the one household of God. The conflicting diversity of our human hopes can be acknowledged and integrated because such communities are held together not by a common conviction or commitment to a common cause, but by the power of God's Spirit. They are inclusive communities in which all can find their place irrespective of age, gender and status. And precisely because they are able to embrace the plurality of human conditions and hopes, they can become sources of hope for the surrounding human community.

Such communities are emerging in many parts of the world. They have become a source of renewal in church and society because they are held together by the one hope which transcends all human hopes and projects. They are free to forge close alliances with groups in civil society struggling to rebuild viable human communities in situations of fragmentation and disintegration. Often they have become the crystallizing point for efforts to build a new culture of solidarity and sharing, of dialogue and reconciliation.

Many churches find it difficult to accept the emergence of such communities, since they do not easily fit into the structures of jurisdiction and the discipline of ministerial orders. The same churches often have great difficulty in acknowledging the plurality and diversity of responses to our common calling. What matters in the perspective of the one hope, however, is not uniformity in structures of life and worship, but the effort to maintain "the unity of the Spirit in the bond of peace". Following the example and witness of such communities of hope, we may find the answer to the question of what it means to be the church today.

6. Vision, Movement and Institution

This book has suggested some elements of a renewed ecumenical vision at the end of a millennium of Christian division, a century of advances and retreats on the way towards unity, and fifty years of the institutional expression of ecumenism through the World Council of Churches. We have drawn on voices coming from the churches and insights gained in their ecumenical encounter to sketch the challenges that face the churches in the world at the dawn of a new millennium. We have looked at biblical texts and images which might illuminate the search for a new vision. In particular, we have explored the visionary implications of the biblical motif of jubilee and of the theme of the WCC's eighth assembly: "Turn to God — Rejoice in Hope".

We shall not spend time here arguing with those "realists" or "pragmatists" who are incurably sceptical of any vision. Mindful of the risks inherent in utopian thinking, we have suggested in the previous chapter that it also has its values. Rooted in the prophetic tradition, the Christian faith holds on to the promise of the kingdom of God. It is thus shaped by an "eschatological realism": it does not have to close its eyes to the true reality of people's lives or to the fragility of creation. It can see this reality in the perspective of God who defends the rights of the poor, the widow and the orphan, the God whose promise to redeem the whole creation is unfailing.

We may perhaps sum up a renewed ecumenical vision in five key terms.

• The ecumenical vision is a vision of *wholeness* and of fullness of life, not only for human beings, but also for all creation (Isa. 65:17-25; John 10:10; Eph. 1:10; Rev. 21:1-4; 22:1-5). This vision challenges all structures which produce exclusion and treat nature as an expendable resource. It is committed to fostering a "culture of life" which rejects the inevitability of war, violence and destruction. The central dynamic of this vision is the conviction that the possibilities of life are enhanced for all when it is shared.

• The ecumenical vision is a vision of *shalom* and of right relationships in a sustainable human community (Lev. 25;

Pss 72; 85:8-13; Matt. 25:31-46; Luke 4:18ff.; Eph. 2:11-22). This vision transcends understandings of peace as security, of justice as quantitative equality and of sustainability as maintaining the equilibrium of the social and environmental system. Justice, peace and sustainability refer to qualities of relationships, and the ecumenical vision seeks to strengthen processes which heal broken relationships and enhance the viability of human communities. It therefore challenges all notions of human rights and human freedom which disregard the common good and the rights, dignity and freedom of others.

• The ecumenical vision is a vision of *reconciliation* (Gen. 33:1-16; Matt. 5:23-25; 2 Cor. 5:18-21; Eph. 2:14-18). This does not mean shutting our eyes to the pervasive conflict and violence in our world or closing our ears to the victims' cries for justice. The vision is based on the belief in the liberating power of forgiveness, which can break the spiral of violence and transform enmity into friendship. Trusting in God's offer of forgiveness and reconciliation in Christ, it supports all efforts which encourage individuals or communities in conflict to turn to each other, to recall together grievances and admit failings, and through acts of forgiveness to accept one another again in community.

• The ecumenical vision is a vision of *sufficiency* (Micah 4:4f.; Matt. 6:9ff.; 6:25ff.; 14:13ff.; 16:25f.; Luke 12:15ff.; 2 Cor. 9:6ff.). It challenges the assumption that only continuous growth will overcome the conditions of scarcity, but lives in the certainty that enough is provided for everyone's need as long as all are prepared to share with each other. It therefore supports whatever enhances the capacity of human communities to become self-reliant, to care for their own needs, to be stewards of their own resources.

• The ecumenical vision is a vision of the *catholicity* of the church as the worldwide community of those who live by the promise of God's kingdom and celebrate the signs of its presence already now (Matt. 26:26-29; Luke 13:29; 1 Cor. 10:16f.; 12:4-31; 15:20-28; Gal. 3:26ff.). This vision transcends the idea that ecumenism is aimed only at convergence and agreement between churches as organized bodies, affirming that a real communion exists among all who confess Jesus Christ and have been made members of his body through baptism. They are not strangers to one another, but members of God's household. As they give shape to their bonds of fellowship, they share with each other as those who remain different but are enriched by the diversity of gifts, traditions and forms of life and witness. Called to one hope, they remain a pilgrim people on the way, anticipating in their life together and in community with their neighbours the fullness of communion in God's kingdom.

Movement and institution

The subtitle of the original German edition of Ernst Lange's book which we quoted in the previous chapter is "What Moves the Ecumenical Movement?". Already 25 years ago Lange had doubts about whether the vital impulse of the ecumenical movement was still alive and began to analyze the "ecumenical malaise". A number of the church leaders to whom I have spoken over the last four years have also expressed the conviction that the sense of ecumenical *movement* must be regained and the institutional captivity of ecumenism overcome.

The tension between movements and the institutional forms they take is of course hardly unique to the churches. Most movements of our century — the labour movement, the civil rights movement, liberation movements, youth and student movements, the peace movement, the ecological movement — seem to have lost much of their vital impulse in the transition to the second or third generation. Some were dissolved because they reached — or failed to reach — their goal. Others were transformed into continuing organizations, such as political parties or trade unions. Still others lost their basis when their goals were coopted by existing organizations.

Movements are goal-oriented, voluntary associations of people who decide to work together in order to change an existing situation or to prevent an undesirable change. They are characterized by flexible forms of organization, spontaneity and a high degree of personal commitment on the part of their members. Institutions, on the other hand, are structures which are meant to provide for continuity. They ascribe rights and duties, roles and tasks, and are expected to guarantee reliability. Institutions are hesitant about change, and over against the idealism of movements, they emphasize the rationality of due process.

To a sociologist, churches — especially the so-called historic churches — are clear examples of institutions. Yet all churches preserve the memory of the early Christian community, which was the movement of a persecuted minority. This movement transformed itself gradually into an institution by developing common structures of ministry and common criteria for the true confession of the faith. Again and again during the history of the church this initial movement impulse has come to the surface — from the monastic movement of the third century up to the Pentecostal movement of our time. All these movements have expressed the impulse for renewal, but none was able to break up the institutional structure of the existing churches. Most were either suppressed, integrated into existing ecclesial institutions or transformed themselves into new ones.

In the long run, all movements are exposed to this tendency towards institutionalization. This is also true of the ecumenical movement. In the first decades of this century it had all the characteristics of a movement. After the founding of the World Council of Churches and the merger of several other ecumenical associations with it, a process of institutionalization began which has been reinforced over the last twenty or thirty years.

Is it therefore mere stubborn nostalgia to continue to speak of the "ecumenical movement" which by now has entered its fourth generation? Has this movement not long since transformed itself into a framework of institutional structures set up to regulate relationships and cooperation among the churches?

Archbishop of Canterbury William Temple, the great ecumenical leader during the formative period of the World Council of Churches, wrote in the prologue to *Is Christ Divided?*:

> Our period of history is marked by two contrasted tendencies — one in the secular, one in the Christian realm. The secular world has lost all experience of unity and can do no more than play with the aspiration towards it. The Christian world is moving steadily and rapidly towards deeper unity, and has an actual experience of Christian fellowship across all secular divisions, which is full of hope for the future of Christendom and through it for mankind.

More than fifty years later, this appears to have been an exaggerated claim. Those excited by Temple's hope for the "future of Christendom" have been roundly disillusioned. Many would go so far as to say that the days of institutional Christianity are numbered. The Christian fellowship today seems to reflect all the divisions of secular society, and in many respects the secular world has overtaken the Christian world in the manifestation of effective unity.

Yet the decisive inspiration of Archbishop Temple, which led to the founding of the World Council of Churches in 1948, lives on. Temple's vision was to see all the major Christian groupings outside the Roman Catholic Church drawn into a worldwide body that would promote fellowship and sharing in faith and witness. At the same time, he wanted the churches to be able to speak and act in the interest of establishing a new international order after the war. He was supported in this by a group of able leaders from the United Kingdom, most notably Joseph H. Oldham, William Paton and George Bell. The wide and inclusive vision of this founding generation reached far beyond the limits of their own context of the British empire, allowing the WCC to grow into a genuinely worldwide body. From 147 founding member churches, nearly all from the historic Protestant traditions in Europe and North America, the Council has now grown to 330 member churches in every continent. The membership today includes nearly all Orthodox churches of the Greek, Slavonic and Oriental traditions and a number of independent, evangelical and Pentecostal churches, mainly from Africa and Latin America.

The distinction between the WCC as an institution and the ecumenical movement has always been maintained. As the fourth world conference on Faith and Order (Montreal 1963) stated, "The ecumenical movement is clearly larger than the Council. The World Council of Churches is one of the manifestations of that movement, but there are many other ways through which the churches are growing together." This broader ecumenical movement has expanded into a network much more complex than Temple and his contemporaries could have anticipated. Not only has the Roman Catholic Church become an active partner, particularly on the local and national levels, but there are now more than a hundred national councils of churches and seven regional conferences of churches, many of them shaped according to the model of the WCC. Through the ecumenical movement, Christian World Communions, such as the Lutheran World Federation, the World Alliance of Reformed Churches, the World Methodist Council and the Anglican Consultative Council, as well as Evangelical and Pentecostal fellowships have affirmed their ecumenical presence. The spectrum of the ecumenical movement also includes a range of organizations, associations, networks and initiatives which are not formed by institutional churches, such as the world alliances of the YMCA and the YWCA, the World Student Christian Federation, the Bible societies, associations of Christian women, initiatives in the area of justice, peace and integrity of creation. The WCC, which its founders proudly thought of as "the privileged instrument of the ecumenical movement", today finds itself placed in the midst of a great diversity of ecumenical efforts and organizations, often competing with each other. Although the WCC is still the most comprehensive of all ecumenical instruments, its Protestant and largely Anglo-Saxon origins continue to shape its profile; and its inclusiveness and "catholicity" are limited by the fact that the Roman Catholic Church is not a member and that the vast majority of the rapidly growing independent and Pentecostal churches remain outside WCC membership.

The nature and authority of the WCC

As the ecumenical movement took institutional form in the discussions beginning in the late 1930s which led to the founding of the WCC, critical issues regarding the nature and authority of the new body — which, despite some parallels in existing ecumenical organizations, was unique in the history of the church — had to be faced.

The very name "World Council of Churches", first proposed by US ecumenist Samuel McCrae Cavert, constituted an innovation, for the World Council is of a different nature from the ancient ecumenical councils or the more recent councils of the Roman Catholic Church. Nor is it a council in the sense of a "church council" as the governing body of a given church. There was also concern in these preparatory discussions that the WCC not be seen as a "federation of churches", in order to dispel any fear that it might, as a relatively small organization, try to exercise authority over its member churches.

The constitutional formulation of the authority of the WCC has remained essentially unchanged since it was drafted during the preparatory discussions in 1938 — namely, that the WCC

> shall offer counsel and provide opportunity for united action in matters of common interest. It may take action on behalf of constituent churches only in such matters as one or more of them may commit to it and only on behalf of such churches. The World Council shall not legislate for the churches; nor shall it act for them in any manner except as indicated above or as may hereafter be specified by the constituent churches.

A prominent question in the preliminary negotiations was whether the Council should have a doctrinal basis. It was finally agreed to adopt the language used by the Faith and Order movement. With the additions accepted at the third assembly (New Delhi 1961), the Basis of the WCC characterizes the World Council of Churches as "a fellowship of churches which confess the Lord Jesus Christ as God and Saviour according to the Scriptures and therefore seek to fulfil together their common calling to the glory of the one God, Father, Son and Holy Spirit".

Two years after the first assembly, the central committee adopted the so-called Toronto Declaration on "The Church, the Churches and the World Council of Churches", which sought to clarify the status of this "fellowship of churches" in two series of affirmations of what the World Council of Churches is *not* and of the assumptions underlying it. This declaration, which is often described as a statement of the WCC's "ecclesiological neutrality", has served to allay fears in some quarters that the WCC might aspire to be a kind of "super-church". It has remained a foundational document despite the profound changes in the ecumenical situation since 1950; and an attempt by the 1963 world conference on Faith and Order to go beyond the understanding expressed by the Toronto Declaration led basically to a reaffirmation of its assertions:

> The Council is not the Church; it is not seeking to be a church or the Church. Although it has a basis of membership which affirms faith in one God, Father, Son and Holy Spirit, the Council does not assume any ecclesiastical authority, nor does it have sacraments nor an ordained ministry. The Council offers itself as a servant of the churches and not of the Church.

Decisive for the new body was its organizational structure and how member churches would be represented and participate in its life. It was agreed from the beginning that an assembly, normally meeting every seven years, should exercise constitutional authority, and that a central committee, meeting annually, would assume this authority for the years between two assemblies. But the formula of representation was the subject of intensive discussions. A regional principle proposed initially was later changed to ensure that the churches themselves would decide about their representation, with reasonable confessional and geographical balances maintained, in the composition of the assembly and the central committee.

Among the various designations we have mentioned (for example, "fellowship of churches" or "instrument of the ecumenical movement"), the understanding of the WCC as a "council of churches" has certainly shaped its institutional profile. The WCC offers the member churches a forum allowing them to take counsel with one another through their appointed representatives. At the same time, it is an instrument serving their needs in such varied ways as studies and material support. Finally, it allows the churches to cooperate in areas of common interest and to have a recognized voice on the international level.

This functional and instrumental understanding of the WCC lies behind the oft-repeated insistence that the churches should "own" the Council. Be that as it may, its specific functions were initially described in only very general terms. Its original constitution said that the WCC was to facilitate common action by the churches, promote cooperation in study, promote the growth of ecumenical consciousness among members of all churches, establish relations with worldwide denominational federations and other ecumenical movements and support the churches in evangelism. In 1975 the fifth assembly adopted a fuller constitutional statement of the WCC's "functions and purposes", explaining the "common calling" which the churches seek to fulfil together according to the Basis: "to call the churches to the goal of visible unity...; to facilitate the common witness of the churches..., to support the churches in their worldwide missionary and evangelistic task; to express the common concern of the churches in the service of human need...; and to foster the renewal of the churches in unity, worship, mission and service".

These statements reinforce the functional understanding of the WCC — an interpretation which has been confirmed by the subsequent expansion of its programmatic activity. As a result, many member churches seem to regard the WCC as a body apart from themselves, which follows its own policies, rather than as a "council of churches".

Organizing a "fellowship of churches"

In view of this widespread image of the Council, it is significant that the process of reflection "Towards a Common Understanding and Vision of the WCC" begun in 1989 has led to a new emphasis on the understanding of the Council as a "fellowship of churches". Of course, the term "fellowship" has a relatively wide meaning, and it was certainly understood in different ways at the time of the WCC's founding when the Basis was adopted. Some would have understood it as an equivalent of the New Testament concept *koinonia*, thus pointing to the essential communion which exists between all those who confess Jesus Christ and who have been incorporated through baptism into his body. Others would insist that the term has no ecclesial significance and that the Toronto Declaration has carefully avoided giving it any specific meaning.

Still, as a fellowship of churches, the World Council clearly aspires to be something more than an association formed by institutional church bodies to serve their common interests. As a fellowship, the WCC must be concerned about the quality of relationships between and among its member churches. While the churches hold their membership in the Council as separate and autonomous bodies, their being in fellowship with one another means that they cannot be compared to sovereign states which hold membership in intergovernmental organizations like the United Nations.

The studies on catholicity and conciliarity referred to earlier enriched the understanding of the World Council as a fellowship of churches. In his general secretary's report to the Vancouver assembly in 1983, Phillip Potter described the fellowship of churches in the WCC as a witnessing or confessing community, a community of learning and sharing, a reconciling and healing community, a community searching to be inclusive and to foster the participation of all members of the people of God.

Does the organizational structure of the WCC facilitate the deepening of the sense of fellowship among the churches? How might the quality of their relationships be enhanced through the WCC? Our earlier discussions about civil society may shed some light on these questions, which of course arise for ecumenical structures at the local and national as well as the global levels.

Most discussions about organizing ecumenical relationships quickly tend to focus on ownership and participation in decision-making and on reaching consensus. Even when it is clear — as in the case of the WCC — that the decisions of a governing body carry only a very limited weight and authority, this "political" logic seems to prevail. Moreover, a growing scarcity of funds has increasingly obliged ecumenical organizations to demonstrate their relevance and effectiveness in competition with other non-governmental organizations. And because ecumenical organizations are accountable to a larger constituency and thus generally have slow and complicated processes of decision-making, they are at a clear disadvantage compared with other partners. In response, some ecumenical organizations have thus begun to reshape their structures and patterns of work to respond better to the specific demands of the economic logic of effectiveness and competitiveness.

The perspective of civil society would suggest that ecumenical organizations should seek first of all to facilitate communication and cooperation among the churches and to intensify their relationships with one another. Earlier I tried to show that the idea of conciliarity in the church, though it also on occasion involves decision-making, corresponds to the dynamics in civil society. The 1971 statement of the Faith and Order commission noted that for the WCC to move in this direction would mean "deepening our mutual commitment at all levels":

> This does not mean movement in the direction of uniformity. On the contrary…, if the unity of the church is to serve the unity of mankind, it must provide room both for a wide variety of forms, and for differences and even conflicts… The churches' unity must be of such a kind that there is ample space for diversity and for the open mutual confrontation of differing interests and convictions.

So far, however, little has been done to spell out the organizational and institutional consequences of this for the WCC.

Furthermore, a new ecumenical reality has emerged in many countries over the past 25 years: at least in the consciousness of church members, the traditional differences between the Protestant denominations and confessions have largely disappeared. Many European Protestant churches have already entered into full communion with one another; and this is likely soon to be the case in the United States as well. In addition, a wide network of partnerships and inter-church relationships has emerged which is not reflected in the way in which these same churches participate in the World Council of Churches. In both the way they act and how they understand themselves, these churches have moved closer together. Yet, in the World Council of Churches, which is intended precisely to serve their fellowship with one another, they participate as separate autonomous bodies.

These considerations support the conviction that the relationships between churches on the local and national levels are the decisive test for their fellowship in the World Council of Churches. As a fellowship of churches, the WCC should give priority to initiatives and activities which aim to deepen the relationships between churches in each place and to strengthen their ability to cooperate in their life and witness. It should thus be interested in seeing that the concern for true communion among the churches is integrated into the programme and self-understanding of local and national ecumenical bodies.

Of course, the World Council of Churches as an organization operates on the international and global level, and while it has to cooperate closely with regional and national ecumenical partner organizations, it must respect their independence and autonomy. At present, no forms or processes exist for formulating consistent and common ecumenical policies between the organizations on different levels, even though most WCC member churches also belong to regional and national ecumenical organizations.

In fact, conciliarity between churches in different national and cultural contexts can less and less be served by centralized institutions and decision-making procedures. If the orientation of the ecumenical movement is to revive conciliar relationships among the churches, then the WCC's role will be more that of a broker or mediator striving to maintain and manifest the coherence of the diverse networks of ecumenical relationships which have emerged among the churches in recent decades.

From the responses of member churches to the process "Towards Common Understanding and Vision of the WCC", it is evident that questions of their representation and participation in the life of the Council remain a matter of urgent concern. They want to be assured that it is truly the churches who "own" the WCC. In institutional terms, this is certainly a legitimate concern; and responding to it would strengthen the WCC's functional character as an instrument serving the churches.

At the same time, what we have said about conciliar relationships — as well as the experiences of the last 25 years — raises questions about whether strengthening the institutional control of the member churches over the activities of the Council will enhance its capacity to foster communication among the churches and coherence among the different levels of ecumenical activity. On the contrary, much evidence suggests that the WCC's institutional structure, with its various levels of governing and advisory bodies, has become too heavy and is not sufficiently transparent for the member churches. Too much energy and too many resources, both human and material, are tied up in processes of reporting and taking decisions which finally have only a limited effect on the member churches. And efforts to strengthen relationships between the WCC as an organization and its member churches contribute little to deepening the sense of fellowship and communion among the churches themselves.

This suggests that, rather than strengthening the institutional forms of the churches' representation and participation in the WCC's life and activities, the Council should rather undergo a certain de-institutionalization, which would encourage member churches to participate in ways other than by sending appointed representatives to meetings of the governing and advisory bodies on the international level. This might also involve steps to decentralize the organizational structure, recognizing that the national and regional levels have become important contexts for ecumenical activity which are not sufficiently linked with the processes in the WCC.

The WCC's functions and purposes should then be formulated in a way that distinguishes between its task of serving as a catalyst for relationships and communication between its member churches and its task of fostering the coherence of ecumenical work on all levels. While the former task is in principle shared by all ecumenical organizations with regard to their own member churches, the latter is the specific responsibility of the World Council of Churches, since there is no other organization which can provide for such coherence. In both cases, however, the main emphasis of the WCC's work should be building relationships, strengthening communication and facilitating the mutual accountability of the churches and ecumenical organizations on different levels. This would require new organizational patterns.

Over the last two or three decades, the WCC has been known particularly through its programmes. Initiatives like the Programme to Combat Racism and the Ecumenical Decade — Churches in Solidarity with Women, as well as the long and patient efforts to work out texts capturing the convergence on Baptism, Eucharist and Ministry, have had a profound effect on the churches' ecumenical awareness and inter-relationships. The WCC's efforts to develop forms of ecumenical worship and to promote the sharing of liturgical and spiritual resources among the churches have had a similar effect. Furthermore, the WCC, as an ecumenical body on the international level, has responsibilities for advocacy and prophetic witness on behalf of the churches on matters of global concern. Two examples from the past few years are the central committee statements on the situation of uprooted people and on the ethical, social and pastoral challenges of the HIV/AIDS pandemic.

In many other areas, however, the most fruitful role for the WCC would be to support and coordinate initiatives whose primary focus is at the national or regional level. Rather than building up its own programme structure in these cases, the Council should aim at strengthening the efforts of member churches or other ecumenical organizations and sharing their experiences and insights further. New fields of ecumenical cooperation which may be opened up and given visibility through a WCC initiative can then be accepted and firmly rooted in the national or regional ecumenical agenda, and the role of the World Council would be mainly that of coordination, sharing information, offering support and facilitating mutual accountability.

Such a new understanding of the functions and purposes of the WCC would suggest that all activities of the Council should be in relation to the purpose of strengthening relationships between churches. Over the past decades, by contrast, relationships and communication have been understood as a support function of the programmatic work of the WCC.

A network with many centres

We have noted earlier that the ecumenical scope of the WCC is limited because its member churches include only a minority — and probably a shrinking one — of world Christianity. This is the case because the Roman Catholic Church on the one hand and most evangelical and Pentecostal churches on the other have not so far seen the possibility of joining the WCC. Relationships with the Roman Catholic Church have grown with the help of a Joint Working Group which was established thirty years ago; and intentional contacts with evangelical and Pentecostal communities have begun more recently. In both cases the present organizational structure of the WCC would appear to exclude the possibility of membership in the foreseeable future. At the same time, the Roman Catholic Church is a full member of almost half of all national ecumenical bodies and of three of the regional ecumenical organizations. Most national and regional ecumenical bodies also include more Pentecostal and evangelical churches than the WCC.

Should the WCC therefore adjust or change its organizational structure to facilitate the full participation of these churches? In fact, several such possibilities were considered in the early 1970s with regard to membership of the Roman Catholic Church. In the end the Roman Catholic Church decided not to apply for membership, and it may be assumed that if these alternatives were to be proposed anew the result would be the same. The model of representation by "families of churches", in which each family is equally represented on governing and advisory bodies (and determines for itself how to work out that representation), which is followed in the Middle East Council of Churches, cannot easily be transferred to the international level of the WCC.

What might be considered, however, is applying this "family" model to the particular area of theological dialogue. It is apparent that the sense of communion and of belonging to one family has been growing steadily among the historic Protestant member churches of the WCC over recent decades; and the Roman Catholic Church already participates officially in the work of the WCC's Commission on Faith and Order. The commission thus includes the three families of Orthodox, Roman Catholic and Protestant churches — as well as, to a more limited extent, churches of evangelical and Pentecostal traditions.

But over 50 years the WCC has developed its own sense of integrity. It would not be easy to set this aside in order to make its membership more inclusive. In any case, we have suggested that the purpose of such efforts cannot be to establish the World Council of Churches as the central institutional framework for ecumenical relationships on the world level. Therefore it is necessary to consider ways other than full membership for manifesting the oneness and coherence of the ecumenical movement beyond the WCC.

The same issue arises for the other ecumenical organizations, which are not and cannot be members of the World Council. National councils of churches, regional ecumenical organizations and Christian World Communions have always been recognized in the constitutional documents of the WCC as privileged partners; and they are invited to send (non-voting) delegated representatives to assemblies and central committee meetings. But there are no recognized procedures to link and coordinate the processes of policy-making and programme planning.

One proposal which has elicited some favourable response is to create an ecumenical consultative forum — of which the WCC would be a member and which would be linked with its organizational framework — to serve the interest of greater coherence in the ecumenical movement. Many existing instruments for coordination, for example, the Joint Working Group with the Roman Catholic Church, the forum on bilateral conversations and the annual meeting of general secretaries of the Christian World Communions, could be integrated into the framework of such a consultative forum.

Many member churches have expressed an urgent interest in working towards a consolidation of ecumenical structures beyond the national level. Particularly at times when churches must in rapid succession send delegates to assemblies of several different organizations to which they belong, and then receive and consider the recommendations of such assemblies, this suggestion deserves to be taken seriously. Even full-time ecumenical staff members of such churches have difficulty keeping track of the array of preparatory materials, assembly decisions and follow-up proposals that results from such a situation. What possible impact can this have on the members of their local congregations? It should be considered whether the constitutional requirements of ecumenical organizations on the world level to hold assemblies of representatives of their member churches at certain intervals could not be combined in a single ecumenical church assembly which would serve the constitutional needs of the different organizations with the same body of church delegates. Preliminary consultations about this proposal have begun. Similarly, more consideration should be given to establishing closer links between the involvement of churches in a given region in the work of the WCC and their participation in the regional ecumenical organization.

Such proposals would of course require much more detailed discussion. But they do indicate that opportunities exist for an organizational renewal of the World Council of Churches which would integrate its work more fully with the life of its member churches and strengthen its ability to serve the coherence of the one ecumenical movement. The forthcoming assembly of the WCC and the 50th anniversary provide the opportune moment to give a new direction to the Council and to strengthen its character as a "fellowship of churches".

However, organizational arrangements must not be allowed to become ends in themselves; their purpose is to help achieve goals and objectives. Even if the World Council of Churches develops a genuinely conciliar form of life and strengthens its character as a fellowship of churches, it must remain an instrument of the ecumenical movement, responding to a vision and a calling which transcend any and all institutional manifestations. The awareness of a common calling is the inner dynamic of the ecumenical movement. Thus, no institutional reform will be successful unless it is accompanied and guided by the effort to clarify and reaffirm the ecumenical vision. This is the most important challenge to the churches and to all ecumenical organizations as we move towards the 21st century.